THE
SUPPORTIVE
CLASSROOM

Trauma-Sensitive Strategies for
Fostering Resilience and Creating a Safe,
Compassionate Environment for All Students

Laura Anderson, PsyS & Jon Bowen, MA

T0040133

 ULYSSES PRESS

Published in the United States by:
Ulysses Press
P.O. Box 3440
Berkeley, CA 94703
www.ulyssespress.com

ISBN: 978-1-64604-045-2
Library of Congress Control Number: 2020931865

Printed in Canada by Marquis Book Printing
10 9 8 7 6 5 4 3 2 1

Acquisitions editor: Bridget Thoreson
Managing editor: Claire Chun
Project editor: Tyanni Niles
Editor: Debra Riegert
Proofreader: Renee Rutledge
Indexer: S4Carlisle
Cover design: Justin Shirley
Cover and interior art: © FGC/shutterstock.com
Interior design: what!design @ whatweb.com
Production: Jake Flaherty

CONTENTS

PREFACE

As educators with a combined 30 years in public education, we have been fortunate to learn from the guidance and expertise of wise and experienced teachers. Our path has led us to work with pre-K through high school students in a variety of contexts, from general education settings to specialized programming for our most at-risk students. The intention of this book is to provide you with a wide range of tools to support all students, especially those who have a history of trauma and adversity. Please keep in mind that all educators have room for growth as we learn new information. We have the unique privilege to make a meaningful difference in the lives of children and families, particularly when we can be more mindful of challenges and supports like those outlined in this book.

As you read, consider small changes you can make that will serve to better support you and your students. There is no expectation to implement every strategy in this book simultaneously in order to experience success. At the time of writing this book, there is a lack of evidence-based, trauma-informed approaches for the school setting. We combined some of the most reliable current knowledge regarding the impacts of trauma with best-practice approaches that are both practical and effective for supporting students.

Warning: This book may connect you to your own history of trauma or vicarious trauma. We certainly experienced this while writing on the topic. Please be prepared, should you need it, to process with trusted friends or family. Be aware of your sources of support; consider more formal counseling or therapy as needed. Another matter to be aware of is that we all have a tendency, when we learn something new, to see it around us. Be careful not to overgeneralize and see trauma too broadly among your students.

PART ONE
TRAUMA IN THE SCHOOLS

CHAPTER 1

INTRODUCTION
TO TRAUMA

When we began working in school systems, the potential immediate and long-lasting effects of trauma exposure and childhood adversity received little attention. Instead, we were trained to identify and intervene with students who demonstrated problem behaviors and learning delays. It is impossible to know how many of those students were struggling in school as a result of trauma or adversity. As well-intentioned educators, we participated in methods that likely did not support these students to the current standard of best practices and even potentially triggered further trauma effects. Thankfully, we have had the opportunity to learn and evolve in our own practices with the support of veteran educators, proactive teams, and professional development opportunities. We have had the unique privilege of spending time in hundreds of different classrooms and have learned practical approaches that truly work in school environments.

Teacher training programs and school districts now offer a variety of trauma-informed or trauma-sensitive workshops and classes. We are collectively improving our ability to identify and support the needs of students who have been exposed to traumatic situations and childhood adversity. Additionally, there has been increased attention on the ways that we can implement proactive behavioral strategies that are effective for all students. Many of these best practices and approaches overlap, and we have gathered some practical strategies together in this book.

WHY DO WE CARE SO MUCH ABOUT TRAUMA?

As our society has become more educated on childhood trauma and adversity, we have realized the implications are widespread and can be very damaging. In his groundbreaking book *The Body Keeps the Score*, Dr. Bessel van der Kolk, psychiatrist and author, highlights, "Trauma remains a much larger public health issue, arguably the greatest threat to our national well-being."[1] As we will discuss in greater detail, traumatic experiences and childhood adversity are implicated in many educational, health, and social difficulties.

According to current data, more than 50% of students in the United States have experienced some form of trauma prior to high school graduation.[2] Some estimates place this number closer to 67% of students.[3] The American Psychological Association (APA) explains, "A traumatic event is one that threatens injury, death, or the physical integrity of self or others and also causes horror, terror, or helplessness at the time it occurs."[4] As we will further describe, defining trauma or adversity is almost irrelevant, as the child's perception of the situation determines whether or not it felt traumatic. Trauma is a perceived experience. We can all agree on the extreme circumstances, such as physical or sexual abuse, weapon violence, exposure to war, etc. However, there is a gray area of what may be considered traumatic, including the perception of what happens in a family, how an individual is treated, how the teacher feels about that individual, etc. Adversity and adverse experiences are often used to describe a wide range of other situations and systemic variables that cause an individual or group stress. Adversity and

---

1 Bessel van der Kolk, *The Body Keeps the Score* (New York: Penguin Books, 2015), 330.

2 "Children and Trauma: Update for Mental Health Professionals," APA Presidential Task Force on Posttraumatic Stress Disorder and Trauma in Children and Adolescents, 2008, https://www.apa.org/pi/families/resources/update.pdf.

3 APA, "Children and Trauma."

4 APA, "Children and Trauma."

trauma may range from lack of food at home to ongoing homelessness to domestic violence to witnessing a school shooting.

Many people who experience what most of us would consider trauma will move forward without significant effects. However, we are seeing more students each year who demonstrate behaviors consistent with trauma exposure. We may not have any information about our students' home lives or histories, so we need to be prepared with a trauma-informed and supportive classroom for ALL students.

Additionally, we believe it is important to more fully understand trauma so we can build empathy for our students who are struggling at school. We have been part of countless discussions and team meetings in which classroom educators express frustration about a student and their particular behaviors. When team members learn of the adversity the child has experienced at home, they almost always feel compassion and renewed motivation to help support the child instead of punishing them. A trauma-focused discussion can help your team move from hopelessness into a problem-solving approach.

ADVERSE CHILDHOOD EXPERIENCES (ACEs)

In addition to trauma as it is defined above, researchers have found that "adverse experiences" in general can have long-lasting effects on children and adults. Since the 1990s, dozens of research studies have been conducted on what have been termed the Adverse Childhood Experiences (ACEs). Scientists from the Centers for Disease Control (CDC) developed the framework for this terminology in the 1990s after they noticed a trend in their data at the Kaiser Permanente obesity clinic.[5] During exit interviews, they began to realize many of their weight-loss patients had experienced childhood trauma, and that excessive weight gain might be related to emotional needs and traumatic exposure. They developed a questionnaire focused on 10 common childhood trauma experiences from the body of previous literature, related to abuse, neglect, and household dysfunction. (See Adverse Childhood Experience [ACE] Questionnaire in the appendix.)

---

5   "Adverse Childhood Experiences (ACEs)," Centers for Disease Control, last modified April 2, 2019, https://www.cdc.gov/violenceprevention/childabuseandneglect/acestudy/index.html.

After decades of investigation, researchers have discovered that the higher the ACE score, the more likely a person is to demonstrate health, behavioral, or addiction problems later in life. These experiences can have a cumulative and long-lasting effect on a person's life. Higher ACE scores are linked to greater risk of cancer, diabetes, substance abuse, brain injuries, bone fractures, and even suicide later in life.[6] Other potential risk outcomes include lack of exercise, missed work, severe obesity, stroke, and STDs.[7]

According to the CDC, most adults have experienced at least one ACE as a child and 20% have experienced three or more ACEs in childhood. Children with higher ACE scores are most likely to be students of color and/or living below the poverty line. As we noted previously, up to 67% of Americans experience at least one ACE during childhood. That number is 83% for people of color.

You may have first been introduced to students and trauma through the literature on ACEs, which brought childhood trauma and adversity to the attention of a wider audience and led to increased professional development on the topic to schools. Keep in mind as you consider your own ACE score and potential ACE scores of your students, this list does not encompass the full scope of trauma and adversity that we experience as humans. The ACE questionnaire does not include many experiences that may be traumatizing for children, such as medical trauma, birth trauma, trauma to the mother while in utero, exposure to community violence, attending a school or daycare with limited resources, having a parent deployed in the military, etc.

Modern researchers and practitioners are clear that the ACE questionnaire, developed more than 20 years ago, also falls short in that it doesn't include systemic injustice, such as "structural racism or heterosexism, transphobia, etc."[8] The standard ACE questionnaire does not include economic hardship, death of a parent, or being treated or judged unfairly due to race or ethnicity. As we will outline in a later chapter, it is crucial to incorporate these factors into our trauma-informed approach so we do not re-traumatize students. Additionally, the ACE questions do not include protective factors (variables that predict successful outcomes) and

---

6   CDC, "ACEs."

7   CDC, "ACEs."

8   Carrie Gaffney, "When Schools Cause Trauma," *Teaching Tolerance* 62 (Summer 2019).

resilience in the score. An individual's ACE score is not the only thing predicting their life outcomes, but it may help you and your team have more empathy when working with students.

REFRAME BEHAVIOR THROUGH THE LENS OF TRAUMA

One of the major shifts in recent thinking has been the shift from believing behavioral problems are innate within the student to understanding the student as a person who has learned to respond to and operate upon his/her environment. In recent years, researchers have suggested, "a primary distinction between trauma-informed approaches versus traditional approaches for behavioral dysregulation is first inquiring, 'what happened to him/her that led to this behavior,' versus stating, 's/he is such a bad kid and needs punishment.'"[9] It is often human nature to assume the worst of others when we are stressed or agitated. Before we began to receive training on the implications of trauma and adversity, and even now when we are triggered, our first thought might be "What is wrong with this student?" when they are misbehaving.

Then, the initial literature around trauma helped us reframe the question to "What happened to you?" Instead of blaming the child for their behavior, we began to acknowledge that a child's behavior is the product of their learning and family histories. Now, practitioners are beginning to shift the question even further to "How do you interpret what happened to you?" How each person experiences trauma and adversity is very unique and is related to resilience and other protective factors. We don't always know a child's history, and even when we do, we do not know how the child interprets their own history. As noted previously, trauma is subjective, and its implications are varying. There is no clear formula for trauma and intervention, so we will use methods that are supportive for ALL children. It is, however, helpful to learn the various trends and themes in the research so we can become more sensitive to our students who may have trauma exposure.

---

9   Isaiah Pickens and Nicole Tschopp, *Trauma-Informed Classrooms* (Reno, NV: National Council of Juvenile and Family Court Judges, 2017), 12.

ACUTE TRAUMA

Many of our students have experienced what is referred to as "acute trauma," or a single crisis event or incident.[10] Examples of acute trauma include the death of a loved one, rape, natural disaster, car accident, or any violent episode. Acute trauma may also include a physical fight or exposure to weapons at school.

Typical signs of acute trauma may include hypervigilance, exaggerated startle responses, overreactions, and misperceptions of environmental triggers. These students may seem oversensitive to unexpected noises or people in the environment. Students exposed to single-event or acute trauma typically return to baseline levels of behavior and functioning after a period of stability. A safe and stable school environment can help the child return to typical levels of functioning more quickly.[11]

A previous preschool student of ours began demonstrating behavioral reactions to any unexpected noises in his environment. For example, if he heard adults talking on the walkie talkie in his classroom, he began crying and asking what they were saying. He flinched and covered his ears dramatically when toys or students made noise. These reactions appeared to have a rapid onset, and the team could not understand where the new behaviors had originated. After meeting with the parents, we learned that his other childcare facility had recently had an emergency fire alarm triggered during the students' nap time. He had been awoken to a traumatic emergency situation and we were now witnessing the aftereffects of this experience. After several weeks of consistency and support, these reactive behaviors diminished and the student demonstrated typical responses to environmental noises.

CHRONIC TRAUMA

Chronic trauma or stress typically has a more significant impact on the brain than acute or single-incident trauma.[12] These situations may include ongoing

---

10   "Trauma-Informed Care Resources Guide," Crisis Prevention Institute, 2017, https://www .norcocollege.edu/committees/care/Documents/Trauma_Informed_Care_Resources_Guide_CPI.pdf.

11   APA, "Children and Trauma."

12   Bruce Perry, "Maltreatment and the Developing Child: How Early Childhood Experience Shapes Child and Culture," presented as part of the Margaret McCain Lecture Series on September 23, 2004, http://www.lfcc.on.ca/mccain/perry.pdf.

sexual abuse, prolonged exposure to domestic violence, multiple home or custody changes, or other forms of child abuse. We have also worked with several students who have undergone chronic and traumatic medical treatments such as chemotherapy, surgeries, or other sustained hospitalization.

Many educators find themselves supporting students who are currently experiencing chronic trauma. For example, we work with dozens of students each year who have moved more than once in a school year. These physical moves between homes, sometimes between parents, and often between curricula at schools, can have a huge impact on a student's learning trajectory. Think about all of the factors at play for a student and their family if they are starting at a new school mid-year.

As with acute trauma, school staff members do not always know about chronic trauma exposure. We typically know if a student is living in foster care or with a grandparent. However, we might not know if the family is living in more than one home or not in a home at all. We have worked with many families who were crashing on a friend's floor or sleeping in their car at night. These families may experience shame and stress about a living situation and not feel comfortable sharing that information with educators. This type of chronic stress can have many impacts, including the inability to focus in class and appearing noncompliant or distractible. Students who have experienced custody changes or foster care may demonstrate a lack of trust toward adults, food insecurity, and increased agitation when someone else touches them or their personal belongings.

For example, we've worked with multiple children who become visibly upset when the teacher attempts to take their backpack and hang it up. We also witnessed a 12-year-old girl with a history of trauma cry and demonstrate meltdown behaviors for over four hours after her teacher unknowingly threw away a pile of shredded paper from her desk. Following multiple moves and family changes, this girl had been collecting her own "personal belongings," and well-intentioned staff had accidentally invaded her personal space by attempting to help her clean her desk.

A student who has experienced chronic trauma may exhibit one or more of the following: numbness, rage, denial, social withdrawal, short-term outlook, or difficulty focusing. We will discuss more signs and common symptoms of chronic trauma exposure in a later section.

CROSSOVER TRAUMA

A less common form of trauma exposure, crossover trauma, occurs when a single traumatic incident is significant enough to cause long-term effects. As we noted previously, children often return to baseline levels of behavior after acute trauma. Crossover trauma is typically observed when a situation involves multiple casualties or victims, such as a mass casualty school shooting, refugee dislocation, or multiple casualty car accident.[13] It is likely that you would be aware if one of your students has experienced this type of trauma.

Over the years, we have worked with many students who moved to the United States as part of refugee dislocation. Not only do those individuals potentially witness atrocities in their home country, they are now in an unfamiliar culture listening to an unfamiliar language. The least we can do is provide a safe and supportive environment in the school setting.

Crossover trauma may result in the following symptoms: mourning, depression, chronic pain, trouble concentrating, trouble sleeping, and irritability.

TRAUMA IN YOUR CLASSROOM

Think of your past and current students and the information you have about their backgrounds. Do any of these traumatic experiences apply to their histories?

IT HURTS MORE WHEN IT'S PERSONAL

Based on all available data, it is now evident that abuse and neglect by caretakers have more complex and pervasive impacts on children than trauma caused by accidents or natural disasters.[14] Consider how many of your students have experienced abuse and neglect at the hands of parents or caregivers. The worst sorts of trauma occur within unhealthy relationships, and it is only through healthy

---

13   CPI, "Trauma-Informed Care."
14   van der Kolk, *The Body Keeps Score*, 145.

relationships a person can heal.[15] When a student has strong relationships and healthy past experiences prior to a traumatic experience, they are less likely to experience long-term negative outcomes related to the trauma. We have a powerful opportunity to build these healthy relationships with students in a safe school environment.

---

15   van der Kolk, *The Body Keeps Score*, 212.

CHAPTER 2

HOW DOES **TRAUMA** **AFFECT** THE DEVELOPING **BRAIN?**

What does trauma do to a developing brain? Countless research studies and new technologies are helping us discover the answers. Understanding how trauma impacts the brain and behavior can help us empathize with our students and develop strategies to help them self-regulate.

LET'S LOOK AT THE BRAIN!

The brain mediates the way we interpret and react to our environment and the people around us. Understanding basic brain regions and functions can help us notice behavioral responses more objectively and use a framework for understanding emergency behavioral responses. Scientists and researchers have outlined three general areas of the brain that we can focus on when trying to understand behaviors: brain stem (survival), limbic system (emotional), and cortex/rational brain (problem-solving/executive functioning).[16]

As we will discuss further, a student who has experienced trauma will likely be more easily triggered into survival state by typical environmental stressors. Similarly, when a person feels that their safety is threatened, their brain is triggered into survival mode. The brain stem activates an emergency response, typically fight, flight, or freeze.

In modern times, when a child experiences a traumatic event or adverse experience, their brain signals an emergency response. The chemicals in the brain trigger the body as if it is in a physical crisis for survival. Over the history of human evolution, our brains have been conditioned to respond to immediate life-or-death threats by going into one of the following "modes":

Fight (react by defending self or fighting back)

Flight (run away, hide, or escape)

Freeze (stop acting, shut down, hope the threat passes)

Each of these modes is helpful when the situation is actually life-or-death or when it threatens imminent danger. However, in modern developed nations, we rarely encounter these threats to our lives. Within the educational setting, these true emergency situations are incredibly rare, but we still see emergency behavioral responses. The student or family may have previously experienced a threatening situation that triggered a fight, flight, or freeze response. Now, when the student feels threatened in the school environment, the same emergency brain response may occur. The human brain is not fully evolved for the modern world and still responds to anxiety and stress as if life is being threatened.

For example, a student may have witnessed a domestic violence situation in his home environment. While his mom was being abused, the student ran and hid in his bedroom. Now, when there is an unexpected conflict or confrontation in the school environment, he attempts to leave the classroom or hides under furniture. He was in an unsafe situation at home and may now feel unsafe or threatened in situations that would simply feel unsettling to other students. This pattern is likely

---

16   "The Conscious Discipline Brain State Model," Conscious Discipline, accessed December 20, 2019, https://consciousdiscipline.com/methodology/brain-state-model.

to continue until he is taught a safer way to take a break and receive support in the school environment.

Our brains and bodies have evolved to respond to trauma and keep us safe. When those efforts are thwarted, individuals tend to experience more damaging long-term effects related to the trauma.[17] Think of your students who have been exposed to situations over which they had no control, such as physical or sexual abuse. These situations are most likely to have long-lasting impacts related to hyperarousal (fight or flight) or dissociation (freeze).

Hyperarousal may look like defiance, anxiety, or running away in the school environment. Students who experience hyperarousal are often sensitive to unexpected touch or noise. Dissociation (freeze) may look like passivity, overcompliance, rocking, or withdrawing. These students might fly under the radar as their behaviors are not typically disruptive in the school environment. If a baby learns that no one comes to take care of her when she cries, she will stop crying and dissociate from the environment. This may look like the child who sits in the classroom quietly, not asking for help or looking around for strategies when she's unsure. Boys and children who are older when they experience trauma often respond with hyperarousal. Girls and younger children often respond to trauma by dissociating.[18]

The emergency response is helpful during moments of crisis but can be harmful during moments of typical stress or anxiety. This response turns off a student's access to critical thinking, causing them to react or act impulsively rather than stopping and thinking. Additionally, we might observe this type of automatic, emergency response pattern in staff members who have previously experienced trauma and adversity.

To address the needs of the brain stem, help students feel safe and free from threats within your environment. A crucial factor here is that "threat" means anything the students perceive as a threat. You may assume your classroom is threat-free, but as we've discussed, a student who has experienced trauma often perceives environmental triggers through a different lens. A seemingly neutral event, noise, or prompt from an adult may feel like a threat to any student with a trauma history.

---

17   van der Kolk, *The Body Keeps Score*, 54.
18   Perry, "Maltreatment and the Developing Child."

Once you address the survival state and students feel safe, you still need to address the emotional state before the students can learn and problem solve. The limbic system is responsible for feelings of love and connectedness. Unless students feel connected to a family or class or teacher, they are not going to be ready to learn and remember new information. A student who is triggered into reacting from the limbic system will be acting emotionally and irrationally. In distress, the child will seek comfort and familiarity. If the individual is familiar with trauma and toxic relationships, they may reenact those circumstances and interactions. Creating chaos might feel safer and familiar, like they have some control over their environment.

Most of our classroom interventions are top-down, trying to talk to students and reason with them (rational brain) when they are still in their emotional or survival states. These verbal and cognitive strategies will not work with a student who is functioning out of their emotional or survival brain. Throughout this book, we will provide you with practical strategies to build a sense of safety and connection for students.

As science has shown us, if we do not first meet the needs of safety and connection, an individual will not be able to learn and problem solve effectively. In fact, a preponderance of evidence has indicated a healthy relationship has the greatest impact on a person's progress compared to any classroom program or curriculum.

When an individual feels safe and connected in their environment, they are able to access their rational brain. They can then make better decisions, focus on instruction, and learn new tasks. Our goal is for students and staff members to spend as much time functioning from this area as possible.

Research shows that IQ capacity actually drops when the emotional or survival brain is triggered.[19] An individual with typical cognitive skills may behave as though they have cognitive delays when emotional/physical safety or connection to others is threatened. It's no wonder we can often look back with shame or regret on our own behavior during situations in which we were triggered into emotional or survival states. In situations of chronic work or home stress, we often find ourselves forgetting information, missing appointments, or losing possessions. We do not

---

19   Erica Van Parys, "The Neurosequential Model and Practical Applications," 2nd Annual Early Childhood Social-Emotional Conference Lecture, December 5, 2019.

have full access to our cognitive capacity as humans unless we are feeling safe and connected.

BRAIN STATE EXERCISE

Again, consider your own students. What behaviors have they demonstrated that might have originated from a survival (brain stem) or emotional (limbic system) state?

WINDOW OF TOLERANCE

Various researchers have started to use the term "window of tolerance" to describe a person's ability to manage stress, especially after exposure to trauma or adversity.[20] Each of us has a range of circumstances and triggers we can typically tolerate in our environment or daily experience. When we are under- or over aroused, we move outside of our window of tolerance and may respond with an emotional or emergency response. When an individual experiences trauma or adversity, their window of tolerance is likely to shrink. This results in seemingly exaggerated or unexpected reactions to typical daily events, as the brain is more easily triggered into limbic or brain stem functioning.

Consider regulation from the perspective that "calm" is in the middle. Some people need to calm down and some people need to wake up or activate. Trauma exposure can lead to the brain either being "stuck on high" (fight or flight) or "stuck on low" (freeze), or it can lead to easier vacillations between the two.[21] If a student is stuck on low, we might observe lethargy, poor attention, and lack of physical activity. These students may seek risky situations and substances and engage in unsafe behaviors in order to activate and feel anything. If a student is stuck on high, they might demonstrate aggressive reactions to minor triggers, excessive motor activity, or hypervigilance in their environment.

---

20 "How to Help Your Clients Understand Their Window of Tolerance," National Institute for the Clinical Application of Behavioral Medicine infographic, accessed December 23, 2019, https://www.nicabm.com/trauma-how-to-help-your-clients-understand-their-window-of-tolerance.

21 "Resources," Echo Training, accessed December 23, 2019, https://www.echotraining.org/resources.

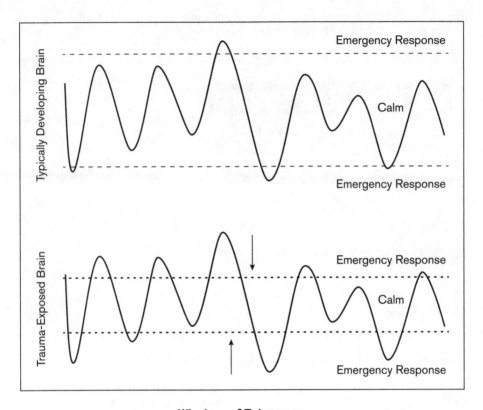

Window of Tolerance

This figure demonstrates how a typically developing brain can tolerate a range of situations and experiences within the window of tolerance without going into an emergency response. When an individual has experienced trauma and adversity, the window of tolerance typically shrinks. The same situations and experiences can prompt emergency responses in a brain that has experienced trauma. A student's window of tolerance can expand or contract each day or throughout the day depending on his level of safety and connection within the school environment.

With this understanding, our goal as educators becomes helping the student expand their own window of tolerance so they can function more appropriately in life and feel safer and more connected to others. Please refer to Part Three of this book for more comprehensive strategies.

THE **SUPPORTIVE** CLASSROOM

THIS IS YOUR BRAIN ON TRAUMA

The traumatized brain can often look and function very differently from a typically developing brain. Recent brain scans of individuals who were reminded of the trauma they previously experienced showed a physical reaction, and those areas of the brain reactivated as if they were back in the traumatic situation.[22] For individuals with fight-or-flight tendencies, the brain responded as if the body were in physical danger. Heart rate and blood pressure levels were also triggered by remembering the event. Others, who have had a dissociative or freeze response, showed very little brain activity or response to the trauma script. It's almost as if those bodies have gone numb to environmental triggers. This may be manifested in the classroom when a student appears to have slow processing speed or difficulty paying attention to important information.

In another study, traumatized children looked at seemingly neutral photographs (e.g., two children smiling and watching their father fix a car) and told stories that ended in negative if not gruesome and horrifying outcomes. Non-traumatized individuals were able to look at the same photographs and imagine positive outcomes for the people pictured. Trauma exposure limits the individual's ability to imagine hope for the future.[23]

TRAUMA AS AN ADDICTIVE CIRCUIT

Another interesting research finding is that sometimes traumatic experiences are able to rewire the brain so that repeated trauma or pain actually begins to feel pleasurable.[24] We see this sometimes to a lesser degree when students find reprimands or negative attention reinforcing, and they increase disruptive behaviors after being praised. Trauma exposure can actually act on the same areas of the brain as addiction, so that pain and trauma become something of an addiction for the body. This plays out when individuals reenact or re-create the same situations they were exposed to earlier in life. Some researchers believe these repeated patterns serve to allow the body and brain to re-create the situation and resolve it

---

22   van der Kolk, *The Body Keeps Score*, 44.

23   van der Kolk, *The Body Keeps Score*, 109.

24   van der Kolk, *The Body Keeps Score*, 32.

with a more positive and safer outcome. It can be our role as educators to insert safety and new strategies into this equation. For example, if a student is running from the room when triggered, perhaps we can teach them breathing strategies and a safer location to run to.

Changes to dopamine transmitters and receptors as a result of trauma can also lead to increased vulnerability to substance addiction.[25] Up to one-half of people who experience severe trauma develop substance abuse problems.[26] Recent research has found that social media "likes" and video game interactions can operate on dopamine receptors in a similar fashion.[27] Consider how many of our students appear addicted to these types of technology use. If you have a student who has access to a cell phone or tablet and you take that device away, you will likely observe withdrawal symptoms.

Some research suggests that increasing the student's serotonin levels can expand the individual's capacity and tolerance for stress and triggers.[28] Medication may play a role in helping calm the brain enough for the individual to learn and practice new strategies. Unfortunately, our society may be overtreating trauma symptoms with medication. Especially for our youngest learners under the age of five, children are ten times more likely to be prescribed antipsychotic drugs if they are in foster care. This approach tends to treat the trauma symptoms without teaching the individual new strategies or coping skills. Regardless of medical treatment, we can provide the individual with a safe and connected environment in which to learn new behaviors and build healthy relationships.

GENERATIONAL TRAUMA

Just as an individual may reenact their traumatic experiences, we often see that trauma repeats itself from one generation to the next if individuals are unable to heal. A recent field of study referred to as "epigenetics" studies the way trauma impacts gene expression in individuals. Scientists have discovered that traumatic

---

25   Echo Training, "Resources."

26   van der Kolk, The Body Keeps Score, 330.

27   Trevor Haynes, "Dopamine, Smartphones, and You: A Battle for Your Time," Harvard University, May 1, 2018, http://sitn.hms.harvard.edu/flash/2018/dopamine-smartphones-battle-time.

28   van der Kolk, The Body Keeps Score, 36.

experiences can impact gene expression for the individual as well as for their future children and grandchildren.[29] Studies have shown that children and grandchildren of war veterans and famine survivors experience increased rates of disease, heart problems, and mental health concerns.[30] This is a developing area of research, so keep an eye on the science in upcoming years.

Consider how epigenetic factors could impact descendants of refugees, Holocaust survivors, former slaves, indigenous peoples, etc.[31] These biological tendencies and maladaptive responses will be continually perpetuated in future generations if we do not intervene and provide safe, connected alternatives to the individual. Epigenetic impacts are just one aspect of systemic oppression facing our students of color and other historically marginalized populations.

Income and parent education are also strongly related to childhood adverse experiences.[32] In short, students who are born to educated white parents who make average to above average income are least likely to experience trauma or ACEs. When we consider this data in light of epigenetic findings, it is not surprising to see perpetuated traumas and adversities in populations with a history of oppression in this country. The APA acknowledges, "There is no doubt that because of poverty and discrimination, racial and ethnic minority youth and families are more likely to be subjected to traumatic events, and immigrant youth and families may be particularly at risk."[33]

Many educators have encountered situations in the education system that are clearly related to abuse and neglect, but this cannot be "proven" through the appropriate legal channels. Cases of child abuse and neglect are often underreported, as claims need to be substantiated before they are counted into statistics. Regardless, official incidence rates are still one piece of data to consider in this larger picture. Official rates indicate younger children are abused or neglected at a higher rate than older children. In fact, children under the age of three are three

---

29   van der Kolk, *The Body Keeps Score*, 129.

30   Olga Khazan, "Inherited Trauma Shapes Your Health," October 16, 2018, https://www.the atlantic.com/health/archive/2018/10/trauma-inherited-generations/573055.

31   Echo Training, "Resources."

32   "Adverse Childhood Experiences," Child Trends, March 7, 2019, https://www.childtrends.org/ indicators/adverse-experiences.

33   APA, "Children and Trauma."

times more likely to be abused than teenagers. These rates are even higher among black, indigenous, and mixed-race populations.

Minority and immigrant students are least likely to access and receive psychiatric support after trauma exposure and therefore most likely to inherit and pass on generational trauma. Dr. Bessel van der Kolk states that "poverty, unemployment, inferior schools, social isolation, widespread availability of guns, and substandard housing all are breeding grounds for trauma. Trauma breeds further trauma; hurt people hurt other people."[34] We need to respond to events with cultural sensitivity when we attempt to support children and families.[35] In school districts all across the United States, Black, Hispanic, and Native American students are suspended and expelled at much higher rates than their white and Asian peers. In fact, Black students make up about 15% of the total American student population, but more than one-third of arrests made on school campuses involve Black students.[36] Imagine how many instances of new trauma we inadvertently create with our discipline approaches.

In the early ACE studies, 28% of women and 16% of men indicated sexual abuse or rape when they were children.[37] These incident rates reflect current reports and may be an underestimate as individuals are not always capable of reporting. Young girls who have been sexually abused tend to experience altered hormone development. They typically develop physically approximately 18 months earlier than peers, which accelerates their hormonal reactions to peers and also may lead to further traumatization.[38] These young women do not have time to heal their own traumas before they become vulnerable to pregnancy.

According to recent estimates, child and adolescent homelessness has also doubled within the past decade.[39] This may be linked to increased natural disasters (hurricanes, wildfires, mudslides) as well as the decreased availability of affordable housing options. Families with children who demonstrate disruptive behaviors are

---

34   van der Kolk, *The Body Keeps Score*, 350.

35   APA, "Children and Trauma."

36   Evie Blad and Corey Mitchell, "Black Students Bear Uneven Brunt of Discipline, Data Show," *Education Week* 37, no. 29 (May 1, 2018): 10.

37   van der Kolk, *The Body Keeps Score*, 147.

38   van der Kolk, *The Body Keeps Score*, 165.

39   "Children and Youth Experiencing Homelessness," Child Trends, May 8 2019, https://www.childtrends.org/indicators/homeless-children-and-youth.

more likely to be evicted. Once a family has been evicted from a rental situation, they are much less likely to be provided another rental opportunity. The eviction on their record prevents them from being approved for future rental options. You can see how this quickly becomes a cycle of adverse experiences and hardship for the entire family, especially if children need to change schools during the school year.

When a family experiences trauma, the adults will likely have less capacity to care for the children. A parent or caregiver who is impacted by trauma will not be able to give his or her full attention to the needs of others. As educators, we can be considerate about these needs and have empathy for families who are experiencing cycles of trauma.

As you can see, our families are often dealing with many layers of trauma and adversity both genetically and environmentally. One of the most promising aspects of epigenetics is that there is potential to reverse or undo the impacts of generational trauma. The body can heal itself and prevent future generational trauma when the individual experiences safety and connection in her/his environment. We can provide this opportunity to our students and families if we are adequately prepared to support them.

HOW DO WE KNOW IF A STUDENT HAS EXPERIENCED TRAUMA?

As we've already mentioned, it is quite likely we will not have a clear answer to this question. The majority of students who have experienced acute or chronic trauma don't meet the technical *Diagnostic and Statistical Manual of Mental Disorders, 5th Edition (DSM-5)* criteria for post-traumatic stress disorder (PTSD), as that definition was created around combat veterans' experiences.[40] Although you may know a student or more than one student with a formal diagnosis of PTSD, it is more likely you know students who exhibit symptoms of trauma exposure but are undiagnosed.

In some ways, it doesn't matter whether or not you know of a student's history of trauma or adversity. The same types of principles and classroom practices can

---

40 van der Kolk, *The Body Keeps Score*, 159.

benefit all students regardless. However, a shared knowledge of the student's previous experiences can help everyone involved begin to normalize their behavior. When other staff members and family members are informed about typical trauma responses, they can understand these behaviors are not permanent and can help shift the child's trajectory.[41]

When we have a student who is frequently disrupting classroom instruction, calling out, and seemingly looking for adult attention, we may label them as "impulsive" and "attention-seeking." These types of labels imply personality traits that are permanent and internal to the child. In some situations, this child might even be diagnosed with ADHD or another disorder and prescribed medication. How might you consider this child and situation differently if you learned that he and his mother live with the mother's abusive boyfriend and the child often loses sleep while overhearing domestic violence late at night?

As humans, we have the tendency to assume a student's behaviors can be ascribed to his intrinsic personality traits. When we approach through the lens of trauma, we can shift our perspective to consider how these behavioral patterns have been shaped by traumatic experiences and can be replaced with more functional behaviors.[42] The next section of this book will provide you with tools to become more adept at noticing signs and symptoms of childhood adversity and trauma exposure within the school environment.

---

41   APA, "Children and Trauma."
42   Pickens and Tschopp, *Trauma-Informed Classrooms*, 6.

CHAPTER 3

WHAT WILL **TRAUMA SYMPTOMS** LOOK LIKE IN MY **CLASSROOM?**

Although a large number of our students have been exposed to trauma, not all of these students have developed severe long-term symptoms. In fact, when students have developed coping skills and protective factors prior to the traumatic experience, they demonstrate fewer negative side effects afterward. We can create safety and connection in our classrooms and build relationships with students to help them develop these protective factors. We can also help build resilience and coping skills in our students who already demonstrate symptoms of trauma exposure.

COMMON TRAUMA SYMPTOMS

In the next section, we will further discuss trauma symptoms as they typically manifest within the classroom. More broadly, trauma and adversity have been linked to the following signs and symptoms:

- Abrupt mood swings
- Agitation
- Anxiety
- Depression
- Dissociation
- Distress
- Eating problems
- Family inability to support child
- Flashbacks
- Gang affiliation or use of weapons
- Hypersensitivities (to touch or sound)
- Hypersexualized behaviors
- Hypervigilance
- Impairment
- Inattention
- Isolation
- Jumpiness
- Low self-worth or self-esteem
- Nightmares
- Numbness
- Regressive behavior or acting immaturely
- Self-destructive or violent behaviors
- Self-harm
- Substance abuse
- Suicide attempts

COMMON TRAUMA SYMPTOMS IN SCHOOL

Common characteristics of students who have experienced trauma include patterns of dysregulation, problems with attention and concentration, and difficulties in social situations with peers and teachers.[43] There are some further trends based on students' particular age levels.

---

43 van der Kolk, *The Body Keeps Score*, 160.

PRESCHOOL

In preschool, trauma exposure may result in increased separation anxiety when the parent attempts to drop off the child at school or daycare. The young child may regress in previously mastered developmental milestones, such as beginning to wet the bed again after being toilet trained. Young children may develop new fears or have difficulty falling asleep.[44] As we previously outlined, children at preschool age are most likely to experience abuse and neglect. These children are also the least capable of protecting themselves or talking about their experiences. Children who attend Head Start pre-kindergarten programming are likely to have already experienced at least three of the adverse experiences included in the ACE study by the age of four.[45] Also recall that if the trauma and neglect are known and the preschool-aged child is placed in foster care, he has a significantly higher probability of receiving psychotropic medication in an attempt to treat behaviors that are likely typical trauma reactions.

ELEMENTARY SCHOOL

In elementary school, common characteristics of trauma exposure include asking questions about or becoming more fascinated with death and dying, starting to challenge authority, and acting jumpy or easily startled. Students will likely also demonstrate increased sensitivity and overreactions to criticism or corrective feedback. This may be the student who pushes his desk over after you point out he has spelled a word incorrectly. A decreased window of tolerance leads to easy upsets and unpredictable triggers in the school environment.

HIGH SCHOOL

Teenagers and older students may also struggle with authority and criticism and may show an increased interest in death and dying. You may notice students having decreased interest in or hope for the future. Early substance use is also often linked to trauma exposure. Students who have experienced sexual abuse as children are likely to be targeted again in adolescence or begin displaying hypersexual tendencies.

---

44 Sheryl Kataoka et al., "Responding to Students with PTSD in Schools," *Child and Adolescent Psychiatric Clinics of North America* 21, no. 1 (January 2012): 119–33.

45 van der Kolk, *The Body Keeps Score*, 352.

OTHER OBSERVABLE SYMPTOMS

PHYSICAL SYMPTOMS OF TRAUMA

Many additional symptoms of trauma exposure may be observed in the educational environment. Researchers are now discovering that children and adults who have experienced traumatic experiences feel physical pain without any clear medical cause.[46] In fact, some individuals lose the ability to use words to describe their feelings but instead feel physical sensations such as a stomachache or cramped muscles. You may notice this symptom in your students who often complain of a headache or stomachache. Often, your school nurse will best know the students who tend to internalize emotions or experience trauma reactions through physical sensations. As noted previously, individuals with multiple ACEs are also more likely to experience diseases such as cancer, diabetes, and heart problems.

LEARNING DIFFICULTIES AND COGNITIVE DELAYS

Traumatic experiences can shape the way our students think and learn new information. For example, some recent studies have discovered a link between trauma exposure and decreased IQ scores.[47] Specifically, trauma-exposed students tend to score much higher on nonverbal tasks compared to verbal tasks. Students who had experienced trauma also scored lower on reading measures and earned lower GPAs. If you consider how trauma affects the brain, these patterns make sense. There is no way a student can pay full attention to instruction and retain new information if he cannot access his rational brain. Additionally, trauma exposure is correlated with more school absences and lower high school graduation rates.

Brain-wave patterns indicate traumatized people struggle to focus on information long enough to retain the information and learn it.[48] Many students who have been exposed to trauma present with symptoms that are similar to ADHD. These students have difficulty paying attention to key details, remaining concentrated on a single task or topic, keeping materials organized, or controlling impulses. Studies have shown the brains of combat veterans experiencing PTSD often look quite similar to the brains of children with ADHD. Unfortunately, these trauma symptoms often

---

46 van der Kolk, *The Body Keeps Score*, 31.
47 Kataoka et al., "Students with PTSD."
48 van der Kolk, *The Body Keeps Score*, 213.

get misdiagnosed in young children and medication is prescribed, but experts are now identifying that "viewing these symptoms as permanent disabilities narrows the focus of treatment to finding the proper drug regimen."[49] These medications do not address the true nature of the problem, the student's inability to regulate their arousal state or responses to threats.[50] As educators, we have the power to address the students' needs from a more supportive and environmental approach.

When a child has experienced chronic abuse and neglect, their sensory integration development has also likely been disrupted. It is not uncommon to see learning disabilities, communication delays, and poor eye-hand coordination.[51] Disruptive behaviors are likely the first concern in a classroom, and after those concerns are addressed, learning disabilities may be identified later. Adults who have unaddressed chronic trauma exposure often have difficulty reading text or following maps.

Another common symptom observed in children who were previously unable to successfully use fight-or-flight responses to resolve problems during trauma is learned helplessness.[52] For example, a student may stop trying to solve new problems because their past experiences have taught them their attempts would not be successful. A student displaying learned helplessness may sit at their desk after worksheets are passed out, waiting for a peer or adult to offer help or provide further prompting.

LOW FRUSTRATION TOLERANCE

One of the most common trauma symptoms we observe in the school environment is a low frustration tolerance. This occurs when the window of tolerance has shrunk and the student is easily agitated. These students often demonstrate volatile emotions and their "first response to new challenges is to lash out or go into defiant withdrawal."[53] Students who have experienced trauma often have altered brain functioning, which means they may go from 0 to 60 with no warning or no clear trigger. On the other hand, these same students may take longer than peers

---

49 van der Kolk, *The Body Keeps Score*, 280.

50 van der Kolk, *The Body Keeps Score*, 109.

51 van der Kolk, *The Body Keeps Score*, 326.

52 van der Kolk, *The Body Keeps Score*, 54.

53 van der Kolk, *The Body Keeps Score*, 341.

to calm back down.[54] Understanding these tendencies can help educators remain calm and provide support while the student experiences agitation.

LACK OF SOCIAL PLAY SKILLS

Another symptom of trauma exposure observed in young children is a lack of play and social communication skills. Many children have only been exposed to maladaptive or aggressive ways of interacting with others.[55] When young children have experienced inconsistent parenting, they are more likely than peers to seek extra adult attention and demonstrate more significant frustration related to small challenges.[56]

READING SOCIAL CUES

Children who have been abused or neglected may experience extreme sensitivity to changes in facial expression or tone of voice. They may perceive a neutral or pensive face as angry and threatening and respond in fight-or-flight mode.[57] On the flip side, some children tend to dissociate or feel numb as a result of trauma. They may feel most alert and activated during potentially dangerous or disruptive situations and appear to have a flat affect otherwise.[58]

LOST WORDS AND MEMORIES

Another symptom of trauma exposure is that the individual does not necessarily remember the trauma she has experienced. We have worked with many children and adults who have been exposed to trauma and cannot clearly identify and artic-ulate those traumas. In particular, imagine a mother who has been a victim of domestic violence and has small children. In her emotional and survival modes, she focused all of her cognitive energy on keeping children alive and often she minimizes or forgets the memories of her partner's abuse. There are many sto-ries of individuals who remember their traumas later in adulthood when triggered during a relationship, therapy, or another crisis situation. Trauma is typically not stored as a narrative in the person's mind, as the language center of the brain is

---

54 Echo Training, "Resources."
55 van der Kolk, *The Body Keeps Score*, 156.
56 van der Kolk, *The Body Keeps Score*, 163.
57 van der Kolk, *The Body Keeps Score*, 116.
58 van der Kolk, *The Body Keeps Score*, 121.

turned off when the emergency response is triggered. Please do not ever discount someone's story if they have never told it before. It might be that they have never remembered it or been able to put it into words before now. In fact, a student may not even remember why they hate the smell of the perfume you are wearing but they are triggered outside their window of tolerance by some previous association.

Children are more likely to forget trauma if they were younger or did not receive maternal support at the time of the trauma.[59] It is highly unlikely our students will be able to tell us about their past experiences. Each year, we also work with students who cannot accurately describe their own behaviors immediately after a crisis situation at school. When the brain is flooded, overwhelmed, and operating out of the limbic system or brain stem, it shuts down language processing. We can accommodate this biological response by understanding that students are generally not intentionally "lying" to us when they cannot accurately admit their behaviors. On a related note, if the student has experienced chronic trauma, there is a good chance they have learned to hide personal or family information as a protective factor. Children in these situations often have a lot of practice creating stories to tell teachers, social workers, etc., to protect the secrets in the family. Regardless, this is how the student's brain has been trained and we cannot take it personally.

In fact, the brain switches from processing and using language to thinking in pictures. This finding has huge implications for the classroom. We can remember that students may not even physically be able to explain what they saw or did when they were highly emotional. We can also remember that students are not likely able to process long or multistep verbal directions when they are anxious or stressed. We can accommodate these tendencies with short, clear directions, visual cues, wait time, and other strategies discussed in later sections.

IMPACT ON SENSORY SYSTEM

Another common result of trauma exposure is that the child loses touch with their body and its orientation in space and time. Additionally, many students who have not experienced trauma also experience difficulty regulating and accessing their sensory systems appropriately. Occupational therapists and experts like Dr. Tina Champagne have synthesized the research on trauma and its impact on sensory

---

59   van der Kolk, *The Body Keeps Score*, 193.

systems.[60] The sensory "powerhouses" outlined by Dr. Champagne impact the individual in the largest ways: vestibular (balance and movement), proprioceptive (sensing the body's position in space), and touch senses. If a student feels dys-regulated in one or more of these systems, they are likely to become much more easily triggered by typical environmental stimuli and experience a narrower win-dow of tolerance. Later in this book, we will provide sensory strategies to target regulation in each of these systems.

IDENTIFYING STUDENT SYMPTOMS

Which of the above symptoms you have noticed in your students' behaviors?

WHAT CAN WE DO ABOUT IT?

It can begin to feel pretty hopeless when we become aware of all the trauma and adversity our students have experienced before they even step foot inside our classrooms. Thankfully, a growing body of research demonstrates that we can diminish potential negative outcomes and build resilience against future adversity. As educators, we are in a unique position to shift our students' trajectories each day. Dr. Bessel van der Kolk stresses, "The greatest hope for traumatized, abused, and neglected children is to receive a good education in schools where they are seen and known, where they learn to regulate themselves, and where they can develop a sense of agency. At their best, schools can function as islands of safety in a chaotic world."[61]

HELP INCREASE WINDOW OF TOLERANCE

A role for educators can be to help increase the student's ability to tolerate stress and triggers. We can provide situations to decrease the student's crisis response. With repeated safe and predictable experiences, the brain can heal. Just as the

---

60   Tina Champagne, "Webinar: Sensory Modulation & Mental Health," Pearson Clinical, Webinar recorded 2011, https://www.ot-innovations.com/webinar-sensory-modulation-mental-health.
61   van der Kolk, *The Body Keeps Score*, 353.

brain can change and adapt when a person experiences trauma, the brain can also change and adapt when the person experiences safety and connection.

We can consider how to help our students turn down their internal emergency response systems. In order to heal, the body needs to become present, rather than focusing on the trauma of the past or worrying about potential trauma in the future.[62]

TRAUMA-SENSITIVE CLASSROOM

A trauma-sensitive classroom can not only provide skills and safety for students who have experienced trauma but can also build coping skills and resilience that can help all students manage and respond to future adversity. The central focus of a trauma-informed approach is to help all students manage overwhelming responses to stress in their environments. These strategies may actually serve as protective factors for resilience during future traumatic events and adversity.[63] When you focus on intentional classroom setup, proactive classroom practices, and appropriate reactive strategies, you can create a safe and consistent environment for all students.

SAFE AND CONNECTED

As we've outlined, all humans have the primary need to feel safe and connected before they are able to learn and problem solve. Students will go to almost any length to meet these needs, and they will often use inappropriate or disruptive strategies until we teach them otherwise. These areas of the brain are developed before we develop the ability to reason and think rationally. We need to focus on helping the student feel SAFE and CONNECTED, otherwise, their energy will go toward meeting those needs. Consider each time you think of a student as "attention-seeking" and shift that phrasing to "connection-seeking." We may need to teach the student a more appropriate way to seek or create connections with others.

There is hope! Humans can actually build new neural pathways in the brain, and we have extraordinary power as educators to support the student with this by

---

62   van der Kolk, *The Body Keeps Score*, 21.

63   Pickens and Tschopp, *Trauma-Informed Classrooms*, 2.

creating an environment of safety and connection. We have the power as educators to build up trust and resources so our students are resilient to future traumas and hardships. In fact, many great leaders have been born out of traumatic beginnings.[64] Oprah Winfrey experienced years of physical and sexual abuse as a child. She attributes her healing and success to teachers who cared about her and helped her find a new way. Let's be advocates for children and learn to approach situations with empathy and trauma-informed practices so our students can recover from trauma and adversity with resilience.

---

64 van der Kolk, *The Body Keeps Score*, 358.

PART TWO
SELF-CARE FOR EDUCATORS

CHAPTER 4

COMPASSION FATIGUE AND STAFF RESILIENCE

Now that you have a deeper understanding of trauma and its effect on the brain, you may be excited to start shifting your classroom and school practices to better support your students. Before jumping into the classroom practices, we want to pause to focus on some important first steps. Too often, schools introduce new initiatives or trendy educational topics to staff members without placing the needed supports to sustain implementation. Educators often forget a fundamental need for staff wellness and self-care. As you work with students who are experiencing trauma and adversity, if you don't prioritize your own wellness, you will likely experience greater difficulty in your implementation of classroom supports.

There are two major reasons to make staff wellness a priority: 1) Educational professionals are fleeing the profession due to stress and lack of support and 2) A dysregulated adult cannot regulate a dysregulated child. If we as staff members are not functioning well, we are not able to operate out of our rational brain for effective problem-solving and classroom management. Teachers are leaving the field with increased frequency, and it's time that we truly focus on the factors involved. You are here to support students, not control them. And you can't support students if you are not first supporting yourself and requesting the support you need. A supportive classroom is one in which the adults are supported first and foremost.

WHO ARE YOUR SUPPORTS?

A supportive classroom is one that has a team or support network behind it. You have to drop any illusions that you need to solve complex problems or support high needs students on your own; you will need help and you will need a team. In this exercise, consider working with a peer or peers, get creative, and brainstorm all the possible people in your support system (possible examples: administrators, counselors, social workers, school psychologists, behavioral specialists, experienced peers, mentors/support teachers, related service providers/therapists, parents, community agencies/partners, paraeducators, administrative support staff, custodial staff, etc.).

If you are working in the field of education, it is quite likely you feel overworked or that don't have access to adequate resources. You likely do not have much control over the system in which you work. You likely do not have control over hiring more staff or more qualified staff. But you do have control over your own self-regulation, proactive planning, responses to situations, and development of intentional habits.

We have worked with a large number of amazing teachers who have worked in the field for 1 to 30+ years. The most effective teachers and school professionals we know have realized that they cannot just keep working harder and spending more hours at school in order to survive. They have focused on their own well-being before trying to instill change in their students. Healthy boundaries and proactive habits will help protect you from personal and professional burnout, and foster your resilience. Since there is no fast-track to create a perfectly balanced classroom, the key will be to maintain your own well-being over time.

BURNOUT

According to a recent education conference, teachers used to be considered a "veteran" after about 20 years. Now, with such high burnout and turnover rates, teachers are considered veterans after three years. We are now experiencing significant teacher shortages across the country and starting to realize there are many valid reasons why educators are burning out. Educators are absorbing the stress and trauma from those around them and do not have the personal and professional support in place to remain employed in the field.

When you spend a significant amount of time and energy supporting students who have experienced trauma, you may start to absorb some of the trauma effects vicariously. This effect is often referred to as compassion fatigue, vicarious trauma, or secondary traumatic stress.[65] Although the terms are often used interchangeably, compassion fatigue develops over time when a professional supports others more than they are supported themselves. Secondary traumatic stress or vicarious trauma can be triggered immediately upon entering a situation in which you are not prepared to manage your own reactions to others' traumatic experiences.

New educators are often surprised by the circumstances they encounter once on the job. Even the best training program cannot create training situations that prepare a young teacher for the first time a student shows up with suspicious marks or bruises. It's impossible for new educators to know how their own body will react when a student shouts at them or throws a chair in the classroom. It takes job experience and hours of practice within context to learn our own triggers, recognize ingrained patterns, and implement new strategies. However, you can spend some time focusing on these areas intentionally and building awareness and proactive habits.

If you want to break the cycle of burnout and teacher turnover, you need to start acknowledging your own signs of compassion fatigue and secondary traumatic stress. Help encourage your colleagues to do the same. Then you can choose from a variety of strategies to seek support and meet your needs.

If you've experienced previous trauma, you may feel re-traumatized by your students' experiences. Even if you have not previously experienced trauma, you may

---

65   CPI, "Trauma-Informed Care."

find yourself feeling similar symptoms to your students—agitation, exhaustion, hopelessness, and depression.[66]

You are at a higher risk for compassion fatigue or secondary traumatic stress if you experience these risk factors:

» Carrying a large caseload

» Coworkers with negative outlooks

» Excessive empathy

» Having your own history of trauma

» Inadequate support systems or teams

» New to your profession/position

» Repeated exposure to stress

» Working long hours

If you are feeling any of the following signs, you may be experiencing compassion fatigue or secondary traumatic stress:[67]

» Changes in appetite

» Difficulty focusing or concentrating

» Difficulty sleeping

» Excessive drinking

» Exhaustion

» Irritability

» Numbness or lack of empathy

» Resentment, pessimism

» Withdrawing or isolating yourself

---

66   Tim Walker, "'I Didn't Know It Had a Name': Secondary Traumatic Stress and Educators," *NEA Today*, October 18, 2019, http://neatoday.org/2019/10/18/secondary-traumatic-stress.

67   CPI, "Trauma-Informed Care."

Administrators and colleagues, take note if you observe any of these collective symptoms on your site or in your programs:[68]

» Apathy toward the school and its mission

» Chronic absenteeism

» Feeling overwhelmed, inability to complete work

» Pessimism about leadership

» Resistance to change

» Struggles within teacher teams

» Aggressive staff behaviors

We will cover strategies for resilience in much greater detail, but here are some things you can do to buffer or respond to the above symptoms:

» Acknowledge or praise others, thank them for helping

» Encourage school counseling supports to lead a professional development session on self-care

» Focus on gratitude during meetings, start with a celebration of what's going well

» Schedule a team-building outing

» Start staff meetings with a mindfulness activity

» Take a walk with a colleague during your prep

Compassion fatigue and secondary traumatic stress do not just impact new and inexperienced teachers. Some of our most skilled or experienced educators often feel the "curse of competence" and get assigned to support some of the most difficult cases. It is especially important for educators to watch out for compassion fatigue as they experience ongoing years of stress and vicarious trauma.

---

68   Jennifer Gunn, "Self-Care for Teachers of Traumatized Students," *Resilient Educator*, March 26, 2020, https://resilienteducator.com/classroom-resources/self-care-for-teachers.

CO-REGULATION

One of the most important things we can do as educators is to build our own calm so we can lend that calm to students when they are feeling dysregulated. As humans, our brains and bodies have evolved to communicate and co-regulate with other living things in our environment. For example, we mirror the breathing of a calmer individual, sense the energy of a therapy horse or dog, and can actually calm our brain functioning in the presence of living plants. Considering this information, it is crucial that educational staff members focus on their own wellness in order to share calm energy with their students.

BUILD YOUR OWN CALM

Before you attempt to build new relationships with students or implement new classroom strategies, let's focus on your own internal state. As we have discussed, very few adults have made it this far in life without experiencing trauma and adversity. All of us have our own strengths and needs, and it is our responsibility to learn them and support ourselves so we can provide the best support possible to our students.

In each moment of our day, we can either bring calm or chaos with our own energy and approach. If we are taking care of ourselves physically and emotionally, we are more likely to have the capacity to bring calm into a situation. When we lose sight of these self-care practices, which we all do from time to time, we may inadvertently add fuel to an already-escalated situation. It is your responsibility as an educator to "build your own calm" so that you can lend it to others in times of need. We will provide many strategies and suggestions to do so in this chapter. You will learn more strategies to build your own calm in Chapter 5.

LEND YOUR CALM

As discussed in Chapter 3, the most important thing we can do as educators is to provide safety and connection to help distressed or trauma-exposed students expand their zone or window of tolerance to stressors. If we can help students experience safety and connection, they can learn that they are able to use strategies to solve some of their own problems. These new safe experiences can retrain the brain for future experiences and build long-term resilience. It is much easier said than done, but with practice we can remain calm when those around us are not calm, and we can lend that calm to those who need it.

LEARN YOUR OWN TRIGGERS

To build the calm you can lend to students in distress, you need to realize your own triggers and develop your own coping strategies. As an educator, you have a responsibility to recognize your own traumas and triggers so you do not project those needs and that energy onto your students. Consider the ACEs discussed in Chapter 1.

PERSONAL ACEs

What was your own personal ACE score?

What other forms of trauma and adversity have you experienced in your life? What is your history of experiencing vicarious trauma in your professional life? All of these factors will impact the way you approach your students and handle stressful situations.

The human experience is full of adversity and joy and trauma and recovery. You are full of triggers and emotions, and sometimes you learn about these patterns and tendencies the hard way. Knowing these things about yourself can help you understand why certain student behaviors or situations are more likely to trigger you than others. You are not expected to feel or even act completely calm 100% of the time every single school day. It is irrational to expect that of yourself or your colleagues. Truthfully, it is amazing and professional when you can identify your own emotions and triggers and request help or a break when needed. Understand when you need to walk away from a situation because you are unable to bring calm, and learn your nearby supports so you can request classroom coverage or a break or extra supervision for a situation.

None of us live and work in a vacuum. Your behaviors trigger reactions in your students, and their behaviors trigger reactions in you. Start thinking about those situations in which you've felt most escalated or triggered, and how your body felt in those moments. Notice those feelings and consider as you read how the strategies in this chapter could be used when you experience that feeling.

Some educators feel especially triggered when students tell them no or are non-compliant with adult directions. Others feel strong bodily reactions when a student runs or darts away from them. Many educators feel triggered when students are physically aggressive, especially when they spit or bite. It's important to under-stand what behaviors feel most upsetting to you so you can identify the feeling and then create a plan for remaining calm and professional.

IDENTIFY YOUR TRIGGERS

Think about the problem behavior(s) that irritate you the most. What does the behavior look/sound like? How does your body react? What sensations do you notice in your physical reaction? If you have a hard time thinking of one particular behavior, try to recall a recent situation in which classroom behaviors became escalated. When did you feel like things were going to get out of control? Has there been a time when you needed to step away from your classroom or a particular student for a minute?

Start to notice: What do you feel in your body when you start to feel anx-ious about a situation that feels out of control? Many people feel pressure in the chest or quickened breath or maybe they even stop breathing. What do you feel in your body when a student yells at you or starts approaching you quickly? What do you feel in your body when a young child runs from your classroom with the intent to leave campus?

Example:

Student Behavior	Your Reaction/Tendency
Whining	Impatience, pressure in my chest

Your body has a natural reaction to the perceived threat in your environment during these situations. You are triggered into an emotional or survival state. Understanding these natural triggers and reactions will help you become more aware of your own calm and chaos patterns.

INTEROCEPTION

Interoception is an individual's ability to perceive how their internal body state is related to emotional experiences.[69] Some researchers argue that interoception is a "prerequisite skill for self-management and self-regulation," as awareness is the first step in making a change or choosing a coping strategy.[70] Considering the variables of co-regulation and your own personal triggers, it is crucial that you are able to pause in the moment and notice if your body is feeling tense and full of stress. If your body is tense, it is sending messages to your brain that you are under threat and need to respond with your limbic system or brain stem. When we carry this tension throughout our day and week, the body and brain experience traumatic stress and health problems.

We've talked about the myriad ways that stress impacts the body. An adaptive or productive level of stress gets you where you need to go and prompts you to get things accomplished. However, you can easily tip over into a counter-productive level of stress, which leads to adverse effects, just like the results of those ACE studies show. If you are living in an emotional or survival state through-out a large chunk of your week, your brain is getting the message that you are under threat and you may begin experiencing symptoms similar to the effects of trauma. Additionally, you are unlikely to respond to student behaviors with a calm approach using your rational brain.

We see a lot of educators who are putting in very long workdays and neglecting their own needs. A lot of young educators in particular believe that they will feel less stressed if they work harder and spend more time on lesson plans and grad-ing. It's not about trying harder, it's about working smarter and interrupting the threat response from your body to your brain.

You can develop and practice interoceptive awareness, building your capacity to notice changes in your own heartbeat, breathing, and muscle tension. Scan your body frequently and notice any tension you can release. Researchers indicate this practice can help individuals respond to agitation with both logic and emotions, more from the rational brain than out of the brain stem.

69   "Interoception," Government of South Australia, Department for Education, February 2019, https://www.education.sa.gov.au/supporting-students/health-e-safety-and-wellbeing/health-support-planning/managing-health-education-and-care/neurodiversity/interoception.
70   Government of South Australia, "Interoception."

When you can intercept the message/threat response and relax your muscles in order to bring yourself back to calm, then you can make a choice to respond from your rational brain rather than react from your limbic system or brain stem. You can take two minutes to do deep breathing, or if you are in the middle of a conversation you can do a quick check-in with your body to see how you're feeling. Release tension in your jaw or shoulders. Practice these strategies at least twice a day every day so they are accessible to you when you feel triggered.

INTEROCEPTION ACTIVITY EXAMPLE

Here is an example of an interoception activity provided by the Department of Education in Australia:[71]

» Sitting down with your hands resting on your lap, notice how your hands feel when they are relaxed.

» Now, stretch your fingers as wide apart as possible and hold them tense like that for 30 seconds.

» In what part of your hand could you feel the stretch?

» Repeat the activity. This time, when you stretch your fingers, focus on the webs of your fingers.

» Repeat the activity again.

» How did the webs of your fingers feel? What did you notice?

Using an interoception activity to ground yourself brings you back to the present moment and orients your body in time and space. One school principal mentioned that she put a rubber band on her left wrist in the morning, and each time she checked in with herself using an interoception activity she moved it to the other wrist. There are days when that rubber band had never been moved. She could then reflect that maybe she wasn't making decisions from her "best self" that day. This practice of interoception will interrupt the threat response your body tension is sending to your brain and will lead to better overall wellness.

---

71   Government of South Australia, "Interoception."

CHAPTER 5

BUILD YOUR OWN **CALM**

In order to build your calm and your capacity to use interoception and other strategies in the moment, you need to spend time building your calm at home and at school. In this section, we will offer a variety of strategies we have either used personally or learned from wiser and more experienced educators. Making self-care a priority can help you build more capacity to provide safety and connection for students, as well as maintain your own physical and mental health. At the end of this chapter, there will be a space for you to reflect on your own practice of building calm.

SELF-CARE TO BUILD CALM OUTSIDE OF WORK

You won't have the capacity to function in your rational brain and choose appropriate strategies in the moment if you are not taking care of yourself outside of work. You can improve your mood and overall functioning by shifting habits even just slightly. You have to build up your calm so that you can access it when you really need it. We know that time is limited and all of these habits take time, but it's your choice whether you will spend time and money on preventative or reactive care. In fact, as wellness educator Joyce Sunada points out, "If you don't take time for your wellness, you will be forced to take time for your illness."[72] This notion applies equally to physical and mental health. Unfortunately, many of you push so hard to get work done and support students that you end up with unexpected medical or mental health needs. When you focus on self-care, you are actually expanding your own window of tolerance so you are less likely to be triggered into an emotional or survival state.

GET PHYSICAL EXERCISE

You've heard it before. Physical exercise is good for you in almost every way. However, you still haven't been able to make it a consistent priority because you're exhausted after work and you have other obligations, or maybe there's a lingering injury from the last time you overexercised. We get it. There are days when we plan to go to the gym after work but just don't feel motivated at the end of the school day. There are other days when we intend to wake up early to go for a neighbor-hood run, but then the alarm rings and the bed just feels so cozy and warm. Keep finding ways in which you enjoy moving your body and then set yourself up for greater success.

Maybe you realize you enjoy walking much more than running, and you can increase your likelihood of getting out of bed for a walk if you place warm athletic wear next to your bed the night before. Keep a packed gym bag in your car in case the opportunity and motivation arise after work one day. Try yoga as a great physical activity that also adds an element of emotional wellness and stress relief. Yoga also provides extra practice in the area of interoception (increased body awareness). Find a new gym or exercise class, or an accountability buddy who will meet you at the gym or trailhead at a certain time. Or, even better, set yourself up on a reward system where you can earn a certain outing or privilege or item if you meet your exercise goal for the week or month. The key here is not to focus on a certain calorie burn or weight-loss goal, but rather exercise for the natural endorphins and lasting mood boost that results from physical activity.

---

72   Joyce Sunada, "The Ripple Effect of Teacher Wellness: Taking Time Out for Your Wellbeing," Thompson Books webinar, accessed December 24, 2019, http://thompsonbooks.com/kto12/h/huddle/ripple-effect.

GET OUTSIDE

If you want to maximize the emotional and mental benefits of your workout, exercise in nature! Related to co-regulation with other living things, researchers are finding fascinating outcomes in the brains of people who walk in nature or among greenery without using technology. These people are more focused, calm, and able to concentrate on tasks after nature exposure.[73] We personally love to spend time camping and hiking as an escape from work and other pressures. It's especially helpful when we can explore a place without phone service, as it forces us to be more present and completely disconnect. We have colleagues who make it a point to go for a walk outside during their lunch break or prep time. This quick reset can be especially helpful for those of you who do not have windows to the outside in your work areas or classrooms.

OUTDOOR ACTIVITIES

Think about the types of physical exercise you enjoy or that help build your calm. Try to add at least one outside activity to this list to get your fix of nature.

NOURISH YOURSELF

You may tend to feel overwhelmed and pressed for time after work, so you pick up dinner or snacks at the drive-through. It's common to crave unhealthy foods full of carbohydrates and fats during times of stress. You may notice your mood and energy levels diminishing if you are overindulging in these types of foods. Additionally, these expenses tend to accumulate and add to financial stress for already-underpaid educators. If you want to decrease these impulsive food choices, consider keeping a stash of affordable and preferred snacks in your car and a few easy and comforting meal options at home.

---

73 Florence Williams, *The Nature Fix: Why Nature Makes Us Happier, Healthier, and More Creative* (New York: W. W. Norton, 2017).

On a related note, educators often find themselves drinking alcohol socially and/or to cope with work-related stress. Consider your current use of alcohol and other substances and whether it is serving to build your calm.

✋ HEALTHY SNACKS LIST

Take a few minutes to make a shopping list, either here or electronically, of your favorite snacks to keep on hand at home, in your car, or in your classroom.

_____

_____

_____

_____

_____

_____

_____

_____

_____

MAINTAIN SOCIAL CONNECTIONS

It's really easy to get caught up in a work-and-home responsibility loop and neglect your social connections and relationships. Think about friends and family members who tend to bring you energy and peace. Contact them and get something on the calendar so it will actually happen. One of our colleagues pointed out that she noticed work obligations were often written in pen on her calendar while personal appointments and fun activities were penciled in and more likely to be canceled or changed. We have learned to set up hikes, happy hours, yoga classes, and even just working lunches with friends weeks in advance so these social activities have priority on the calendar. In our house, we like to put trips and adventures on the calendar to give us something to look forward to when we are stressed. Sometimes, you may dread leaving your house when the day actually arrives, or you may feel like you have too many things to get done instead, but you will rarely regret quality time spent with others. These activities can help you build calm as well as expand your own window of tolerance for stress and triggers. Healthy relationships and social connections are most predictive of our happiness as children and adults.

FRIENDS AND COLLEAGUES LIST

Take a few minutes to make a list of people who tend to bring you peace or positive energy when you spend time with them. Reach out to one or more of them to set up plans in the upcoming weeks.

CARVE OUT PERSONAL TIME AND SPACE

On the other hand, if you find yourself feeling drained by social obligations and pressure from your calendar, intentionally carve out some down time. It is completely healthy and acceptable to realize you are feeling overwhelmed and to set boundaries to prevent additional plans and obligations. Notice when your body needs to slow down, and tell people no when they ask for a favor or to make plans. This is often especially hard for many educators, as we feel compassion for others and want to offer our help to friends and colleagues in need. Think of setting boundaries as a matter of protecting your own energy and time rather than a matter of letting someone else down. Find a simple routine that helps you feel grounded and centered in your own personal time: journaling, gardening, taking a bath, getting a pedicure, reading, listening to music, cleaning, etc. Simple and repetitive activities can help ground you and restore your calm.

What types of activities do you find valuable to incorporate into your personal habits? What household or neighborhood tasks help you feel grounded and calm? Make a quick list.

_____

_____

_____

_____

_____

CONSIDER MEDITATION/MINDFULNESS

Meditating for 20 minutes per day makes a significant impact on a caregiver or teacher's effectiveness to support students with challenging behaviors. In fact, appropriate behaviors increase greatly while problematic behaviors decrease greatly. This is in comparison to similar situations in which the adult does not meditate but uses the same behavioral approaches in the classroom.[74]

One research study followed preschool classroom behaviors while teachers attended an eight-week mindfulness course.[75] During and following the eight-week course, challenging student behaviors and negative peer interactions decreased. Compliance with adult directions and appropriate individual play skills increased. A meta-analysis of related literature found that caregiver or teacher mindfulness is linked to increased progress on IEP goals, decreased student aggression, fewer

74   Nirbhay Singh, "Mindfulness-Based Positive Behavior Support (MBPBS)," presentation accessed December 24, 2019, https://hcpbs.files.wordpress.com/2017/10/mindfulness-based-pbs.pdf.

75   Nirbhay Singh et al., "Mindfulness Training for Teachers Changes the Behavior of Their Preschool Students," _Research in Human Development_ 10, no. 3 (2013): 211–33.

physical restraints, and lower rates of staff burnout.[76] It seems almost unbeliev-able that an adult's energy can have such a large impact on student behavior, but it also highlights how much power you hold as educators when you are able to build your own calm.

MEDITATION EXERCISE

Consider investigating meditation techniques if you do not already have a meditation practice, to see if it's for you. Look into apps for your phone and other guided meditations online. Many of these resources are free and a great place to start your practice. Keep in mind that, like almost anything else, the key is to continue practicing day after day or week after week, even if for only a few minutes a day.

PRACTICE GRATITUDE

Related to mindfulness and meditation practices, many practitioners have begun focusing on the practice of intentional gratitude. Countless studies have indicated that truly focusing on a grateful feeling can improve your overall happiness and even productivity.[77] These studies and researchers have recommended multiple ways to focus your attention on gratitude. Here are some of our favorite, simple suggestions:

» **Count your blessings:** Set aside time once a week or on whatever timeline you choose to sit down and write out a brainstormed list of everything for which you are currently and recently feeling grateful.

» **Keep a gratitude journal:** Some people choose to write one to three things each day in a designated gratitude journal, at the bottom of their planner, or even on a calendar. The key with a gratitude journal is to truly allow yourself to feel authentic gratitude for each item as you write it. This reflection will retrigger the brain chemistry of happiness and gratitude, sending positive messages of health and wellness to your body.

76   Singh, "MBPBS."
77   "Giving Thanks Can Make You Happier," Harvard Medical School, *Healthbeat*, accessed January 7, 2020, https://www.health.harvard.edu/healthbeat/giving-thanks-can-make-you-happier.

» **Write a thank you note:** Take five minutes and write a note of gratitude to a friend, family member, or colleague. Not only will this boost your mood, it's bound to make the other person's day. This can be as simple as leaving a Post-it Note on someone's desk or sending a quick email to a friend or coworker. In Laura's current school, staff members write quick notes of gratitude to coworkers when another person has been helpful or kind to them. This simple practice has helped boost overall staff morale as well as a feeling of safety and connection for adults.

SEEK PROFESSIONAL SUPPORT

It is exciting that self-help and mental health are becoming more openly discussed in friend groups and in our society. Hopefully, this trend will help people further drop the stigma around seeking therapy and professional mental health supports. As you read and learn more about trauma and adversity, you may recognize some personal patterns and experiences in your own life. You may also realize that you are often triggered by particular situations and would like to learn additional coping skills and strategies. As needed, consider visiting with a counselor or therapist, joining a support group in your area, or accessing spiritual guidance through your community or church. Offer yourself the same support you offer and wish for others.

SELF-CARE TO BUILD CALM AT WORK

You can do many things outside of work to focus on self-care and overall wellness, but it is also important to focus on your workday and how you build calm and manage emotions in that environment. Many educators spend more waking hours at school than anywhere else during the work week. Find ways to build calm and peace into your work routines so you can feel better and be more effective in your practices.

CREATE A CALM WORK ENVIRONMENT

What is your gut feeling when you walk into your classroom or office? Do you feel calm and centered or do you feel pressured and anxious? Just like human energy, a physical space can feel either calm or chaotic. Some of these reactions may not be within your control but rather linked to previous experiences and memories within that environment. However, there are many aspects you CAN control in your environment. Consider lighting options and furniture arrangement. If you are allowed, bring lamps or alternative lighting to shift away from the intensity of fluorescent lights. When not allowed to bring in additional electric devices, some staff members have submitted work orders to have half of the fluorescent light bulbs removed. This can change the entire atmosphere of a classroom or workspace.

Intentionally build a small area or space in your room that brings you joy. If you have a happy place, frame a picture of it on your wall or make it your laptop background. Post photographs, inspiring or humorous quotes, and personal artifacts from your life outside of the classroom. These reminders can also help you gain perspective when you feel trapped in an overwhelming situation. Bring live plants into your classroom if at all possible. As we previously discussed, there is fascinating research to support that co-regulation with living plants can actually build calm and increase a person's window of tolerance.[78]

Consider a simple routine to follow each day, such as making a daily list or cleaning your desktop or work area before the school day or before you leave for home each afternoon/evening. This can reduce the amount of anxiety you experience at the beginning of the next day and set you up for a calmer welcome back to the educational environment. You may get into the habit of arriving for work with just enough time ahead of morning appointments or student arrival, but if you can instead arrive a few minutes before others, this can also be a calming way to enter the school day.

WORK SPACE EXERCISE

How could you improve your workspace to foster a sense of calm? What could you add? What could you remove? Take a minute to generate some ideas and add them to your to-do list.

---

78 Min-Sun Lee et al., "Interaction with Indoor Plants May Reduce Psychological and Physiological Stress by Suppressing Autonomic Nervous System Activity in Young Adults: A Randomized Crossover Study," *Journal of Physiological Anthropology* 34, no. 21 (April 28, 2015), https://jphysiolanthropol.biomedcentral.com/articles/10.1186/s40101-015-0060-8.

REMEMBER TO BREATHE

When the body experiences anxiety or distress, breathing patterns often change automatically. Many people actually stop breathing or hold their breath when they feel stressed. This happens naturally but can be quite destabilizing. You need to keep breathing in order to move oxygen to your brain as you are attempting to make decisions about how to respond. Find a way to remind yourself to keep breathing when you are in a stressful situation. We've seen some teachers put a visual cue on the wall of the classroom or on the corner of a laptop screen. Maybe it's actually the word "breathe," or maybe it is a more subtle cue such as a peaceful landscape scene or a balloon or anything else that reminds you to take a deep breath. This is such a simple reminder, but so often overlooked in moments of stress. The more you practice interoception, the more quickly you will notice these tendencies in your own body.

NOURISH YOURSELF

Another thing educators tend to overlook is their own need for food and water during the school day. How many times have you skipped lunch because you needed to make copies or make that parent phone call? Quit putting other people's needs before your own! You need to eat or you will inadvertently bring chaos into some afternoon interactions. Ideally, you would have time to meal prep healthy lunches on Sunday and bring them to work so you are full of amazing nutrients and vitamins throughout the week. Maybe instead, you get "Sunday scaries" like many of us and begin ruminating or worrying about the week instead of packing meals on Sunday evening. Or, you have countless other responsibilities in your life and family needs that inhibit your ability to leisurely create proactive, healthy meals. In our experience, it is helpful to stock up on granola bars, dried fruit, bottled water, and other nonperishable items to keep on hand in your classroom for those days when things just don't go as planned. Also, these snacks can be helpful to have on hand for your students who come in hungry and can't focus until they eat.

SNACK LIST

If you didn't before, take a minute to add some healthy and/or quick snacks to your shopping list!

PUT STRESS ON PAUSE

As much as possible, try to keep work stress at work and home stress at home. Obviously, as all humans do, you will experience the highs and lows in both environments, and this fluctuation may impact your energy as you transition back and forth. Consider how your energy is impacted when you are running late or have a morning conflict in your family or you forget your coffee at home. By the time you get to school, you cannot go back and undo what has been done. The healthiest thing you can do is attempt to let it go and move forward with your day. Easier said than done. The same is true in reverse, when you have a stressful day at work and let that energy carry over into your evening. Perhaps you email or text with coworkers in the evening to vent and debrief. All of this negative energy is bleeding over into your free time and time for which you are not being paid to work. Consider if you would like to set some boundaries in this area. We have worked with many professionals who have come up with the following creative strategies:

» Find a milestone on your commute where you can visualize leaving stress behind you. For example, "When I pass that sign by Exit 32 on the way to work, I'm going to switch my focus to the school day. When I pass the same sign on the way home, I will switch to my home life and family/friends."

» One colleague visualized hanging work stress in the tree outside his garage when he arrived home each day.

» Consider not checking notifications on your phone while at work unless they are related to family emergencies (WAY easier said than done in today's society). On the flip side, consider setting a time after which you will not communicate electronically with coworkers about work-related issues. Some colleagues have chosen 7 p.m. as their cutoff for work correspondence and then 10 p.m. as their cutoff for any technology use.

» One of our veteran teachers mentioned that she would stop and think before she shared any stories about work with her husband. She would ask herself, "Will sharing this story make me laugh or smile?" If the answer was no, she stopped herself from repeating the story.

Some veteran educators take some time immediately upon arriving home from work to decompress before rolling into the evening routine. Take a few minutes to sit alone, listen to music, meditate, or whatever works for you. This pause can prevent bringing negative energy or reactive responses into your home environment. Allow the energy of the day to release or integrate before you move into the rest of your evening.

PLAN BREAKS AND REWARDS

Just like you do for students who need a little extra encouragement, set up contingencies for yourself as you complete work, especially when you have difficulty remaining motivated and focused. For example, we both worked on this book while camping, with the goal to meet a writing goal each day before hiking. We have known teachers who make contracts with themselves to go for a 10-minute walk outside during their prep period after entering so many grades or preparing a certain amount of materials. Special education teachers may reward themselves with a fancy coffee to enjoy while writing a difficult individualized education program (IEP). If you know you have a potentially contentious meeting on your calendar, schedule a fun or relaxing activity for afterward (e.g., first meeting, then happy hour).

On a related note, build breaks into your life! There is no reason to force yourself to complete all of a task within one chunk of time if you can break it into smaller chunks and get some movement in between these times. Your brain will function much more efficiently, the quality of your work will improve, and you will feel less emotional and cognitively drained as a result.

CONSULT WITH COWORKERS AND OTHER PROFESSIONALS

It is so easy in the school environment to either isolate yourself or find yourself surrounded by colleagues with negative outlooks. Take a look at the people you tend to spend the most time with at work, and think about whether you feel energized or drained after interactions with those people. Consider additional colleagues and professionals with whom you could consult or socialize. Education professionals are often more than willing to offer support, listen to concerns, or pop in for a quick observation and consultation.

DEBRIEF SOLUTIONS WITH COLLEAGUES

When stress levels are high and support levels are low, it is the perfect recipe for downward spirals and compassion fatigue. It's incredibly easy in a school setting to get sucked into a cycle of negativity, judgment, and even hopelessness. Some people call this getting stuck in the cycle of "admiring the problem." You might start hearing and using some of the following statements:

» If only the parents would just....

» I don't think that kid will ever...

» It doesn't matter what we do here, because it will all just get undone over the weekend/summer...

» He is just so mentally ill...

» With all of the trauma he's experienced, it's no wonder...

Likewise, you might notice staff members who attempt to put the ownership of a child's educational success back on the student or his family. This seems to be a natural and common pitfall that we encounter.

If you truly consider all of the above statements or tendencies, you will notice the numerous ways you either assume children can't actually "get better" or that the child or their family is going to be the impetus for this improvement. It makes sense. It's easier to put the responsibility on someone or something other than ourselves, then we can also place the blame there when the student is not successful. This is human nature. In many cases, it may also feel like you have little or no control over the student's progress. Let's think about how this could end up being a self-fulfilling prophecy. If you expect that the student cannot make adequate progress or change their behavioral choices due to their traumatic experiences or family situation, they are not likely to make progress. In reality, if we help the child to feel safe and connected, they are much more likely to make progress and improve their outcomes.

The next time you or a coworker starts discussing a student in the above manner, think about one of the following ways to reframe:

- How can we provide more support during the most difficult times of day for this student?

- What can we offer as support to the family?

- What more appropriate, replacement behaviors could we teach this child?

- What are our goals for this student? What goals does the family have? What are the student's goals?

- What's one small change we could make to support them?

As much as possible, try to redirect the conversation toward problem-solving rather than complaining. This will help staff remain calmer and also build more hope for the student to make progress.

ASK FOR HELP OR A BREAK

The first step to making any changes is to realize what is currently happening. Recall our exercise on triggers and/or the most recent situation in which you interacted with an escalated individual. What happened first? What did you do next? How did the student respond in reaction to your behavior? It is likely that you do not recall all of the details or even what your body did and said in the moment. As we described in Chapter 2, the language center of the brain tends to shut down when a person is flooded with emotions. That impacts your memory of what was said and done while you were emotional. If you are unable to dissect a recent situation from memory, consider asking other staff members who may have observed the incident for their perspective on what happened.

When you start to notice your own behavioral patterns, you can cue your colleagues to help prompt you and remind you of choices. We have worked with many teams who come up with creative ways to keep each other professional and calm during a crisis. Some teams will cue each other to get a drink of water or "take a phone call in the office" as a code for "you need a break." Other teams have used codes such as, "I need a drink of water," or "They need you in room 15" to cue each other that someone else needs to work with this child since the situation is currently escalating. For example, in one of our programs, staff members have utilized the American Sign Language gesture for "help" to indicate to other staff members they need assistance. Any of these strategies are subtle cues that do not let the student see you are in distress or triggered into an emotional or survival state. If we can let go of our ego's need to manage the situation, we can realize this isn't about our needs but about keeping the child safe and connected. At times, that requires a change in staff or a change in strategy. We will dive much deeper into proactive and reactive behavioral strategies in upcoming sections.

What is your first reaction when you think about people who "need" help from others? Do you think less of a person who requires support to accomplish tasks? Do you feel judgmental toward others who are unable to do their jobs as well as you do yours? If so, you may feel less likely to ask for help yourself. It is crucial for all educators to acknowledge that everyone needs help with something. The sooner you can feel comfortable with receiving help, the sooner you can offer genuine help to others.

TAKE SOCIAL MEDIA CHALLENGES

Some teachers and principals have created social media challenges for teachers to address aspects of self-care. They challenge teachers to choose at least one thing from the list and post a photo of it on Instagram or Facebook. You could start something like this with your staff, creating safety and connection between the adults. Some suggested staff challenges are:

» Leave school on time one or two days a week.

» Leave your teacher work bag at school one or two days a week.

» Exercise or go to the gym after school, ideally with a friend for social connection.

» Treat yourself to something special once a month, such as a pedicure, fancy coffee, movie, etc.

» Say "no" to something extra that someone asks you to do.

If your colleagues do not connect on social media, this type of challenge could also be held over work email or on a bulletin board in the staff workroom or break area.

CELEBRATE SUCCESSES

Make it a point to start staff meetings, team meetings, and meetings with parents by talking about recent successes. Stay focused on what is going well for the first few minutes of the meeting, and notice how that shifts the morale and relieves the anxiety of participants. With colleagues, it can help your team realize that some things are actually going well when situations feel overwhelming or hopeless. With parents and families, you will help them relax and feel welcome on the team by communicating the things you love or enjoy about their student. This is a small but powerful tweak to begin implementing as a habit.

In addition, plan staff celebrations that are not necessarily linked to achievements or progress. Some schools have a monthly potluck to celebrate birthdays, others hold happy hours or pizza parties each quarter for social connections. Classroom teams may decide to perk up a morning brainstorm session with donuts and coffee from off-campus. Think about ways that you can build these celebrations into your team schedules or suggest them to your site administrators for broader effects.

LOOK INTO PROFESSIONAL DEVELOPMENT

If you are starting to feel burned out in your classroom or office, look into professional development opportunities that spark your interest. Maybe you will find a new approach or strategy to implement, or maybe you will find a new area of passion or research. It's also likely you will learn that you are already doing many positive and proactive things for your students. Continued learning can help you feel regenerated or encouraged in your professional practices.

STAFF CHALLENGES AND CELEBRATIONS

Think about the team of people you work with on a regular basis. How can you create a challenge for all of you to focus more on self-care? What kinds of celebrations could you schedule? Jot down some ideas here!

_____

_____

_____

_____

_____

KEEP IT IN PERSPECTIVE

You are not expected to be everything to everyone. You are not responsible to fix or save anyone. Try to remain focused on the things over which you have some control. You are only responsible to build your own calm so you can lend it to others while they heal and learn to solve their own problems. People begin to feel compassion fatigue when they feel the need to be more helpful to more people or in more situations than they can possibly manage individually. In fact, we often begin to feel guilty for not doing more in situations where we have maybe already crossed the line into helping too much.

There are other ways to keep yourself in check and keep perspective on problems that arise within your school day. Over the past several years, we've heard from veteran teachers who use the acronym QTIP to remind themselves and their team members to "quit taking it personally." Some educators even tape a cotton swab to the wall or leave one on their desk as a cue.

PLAN TO BUILD YOUR OWN CALM

In our experience, it was very difficult to manage our own emotions and responses to triggering situations at the beginning of our careers. We were likely to feel anxious or angry or hopeless in reaction to student behavior at times. We certainly responded in ways that were overreactive and at times put ourselves and the students at greater risk of physical or emotional danger. As the years have gone by, in addition to learning more effective practices, we have become more aware of our own triggers and emotional reactions and can often choose to utilize a calming strategy, take a break from the situation, or ask colleagues for help. However, there are still times when we reflect on a situation after the fact and realize we could've handled things differently. We will never be fully free from triggers and emotions as long as we are human, so we might as well get used to finding strategies and reflecting on situations as they occur. Be patient with the process and yourself. There are no quick fixes, you just keep doing the next right thing.

✓CHAPTER CHECKLIST
Build Your Own Calm

Consider all of the strategies discussed in the above sections, as well as strategies you have discovered for yourself through personal experience. Take some time to complete this plan on how you will build and maintain your calm moving forward.

Home Practices

❑ Get physical exercise

❑ Get outside

❑ Nourish yourself

❑ Maintain social connections

❑ Carve out personal time and space

❑ Consider meditation/mindfulness

❑ Practice gratitude

❑ Seek professional support

❑ Other: _____

Notes: _____

_____

_____

_____

_____

Work Practices

❑ Create a calm work environment

❑ Remember to breathe

❑ Nourish yourself

❑ Put stress on pause

❑ Plan breaks and rewards

❑ Consult with coworkers and other professionals

❑ Debrief solutions with colleagues

❑ Ask for help or a break

❑ Take social media challenges

❑ Celebrate successes

❑ Look into professional development

❑ Keep it in perspective

❑ Plan to build your own calm

❑ Other: _____

Notes: _____

_____

_____

_____

_____

_____

PART THREE
AN EMPATHETIC AND CONNECTED CLASSROOM

CHAPTER 6

EMPATHY AND UNDERSTANDING

With knowledge of trauma's effects on students and the self-care needs of staff, we can begin to build a more comprehensive understanding of behaviors in the school environment. We will discuss how the behaviors you observe in the classroom serve a purpose for the student in the context of their environments, learning history, and relationships.

While working in schools, we sometimes hear staff members make statements like, "If the families disciplined better, or took away technology, or set better limits, the kids would be behaving better in school." It is likely that those variables are impacting the student's performance at school to some degree. The reality is, however, the families and students are doing the best they can at this time in the communities where they live and with the resources they have.

Thinking back to Chapter 2 and our discussion on epigenetics and generational trauma, consider the current family experiences of your students. Many families are experiencing chronic trauma or adversity, including homelessness, lack of food, domestic violence, financial insecurity, mental illness, etc. Other families have a history of generational poverty or racial oppression that has been passed down socially and biologically through the generations.

It is human nature to make judgments about other peoples' situations without knowing all of the details, and we often naturally assume the worst. When a student's parent doesn't respond to an email or doesn't attend scheduled meetings, the assumption may become, "They don't support the school," or "They don't care enough about their child." In all reality, these families may be barely getting by in survival mode or they have their own past traumatic experiences surrounding school. Many of our students who are struggling in school live with adults who also struggled in school. As educators, we may need to shift our narrative to tell a different story about these families.

POSITIVE INTENT

As we move forward, we are going to operate under the assumption that people are generally doing the best they can with the resources they have. Dr. Becky Bailey of Conscious Discipline and many others have referred to this as assuming positive intent.[79] Unfortunately, this is not our typical response. As humans, we tend to give the most weight to, or remember, thoughts and explanations that are negative in nature. This is believed to have served us evolutionarily in order to survive. Researchers have referred to this tendency as our negativity bias.[80] In order to counteract this natural tendency, we can start the habit of assuming the best in others.

Instead of: "I can't believe he just ran out of my room during class."

Consider: "I can see why he did that. He was just trying to escape a trigger and didn't have a better choice available at the time."

In practice, this approach can be helpful when observing behaviors of students, families, and staff members. If a student pushes another kid out of line, you might be able to approach him and say, "You wanted more space. You can ask Steven to move." You start by acknowledging what the person was attempting to accomplish

---

79   "Chapter 9: Positive Intent," Conscious Discipline, accessed January 11, 2020, https://conscious
discipline.com/free-resources/book-portal/chapter-9-positive-intent/#positiveintentsummary.

80   Kendra Cherry, "What Is the Negativity Bias?" *Very Well Mind*, updated April 11, 2019, https://www.verywellmind.com/negative-bias-4589618.

or what need they were trying to meet with the behavior. You can then offer a more appropriate or safer way to meet those same needs.

You can also apply this approach when adults behave in ways you dislike. When you observe adult behaviors with positive intent, you may be able to have empathy or compassion for their situation and the context in which the behaviors occurred. Each student and family is doing the best they can in the current situation, even if their "best" doesn't serve others well at that moment. Instead of viewing others as "bad" or "mentally ill," reframe to view them as people who need to learn new skills or who need more support.

DEVELOP A GROWTH MINDSET

Along with positive intent, approach your students and families with a growth mindset, assuming that individuals and families can change and evolve for the better. Carol Dweck, in her 2007 landmark book *Mindset*, outlined the dichotomy between a growth mindset and a fixed mindset.[81] Countless others have followed in her footsteps, conducting research on these mindsets and further clarifying outcomes. In short, a growth mindset exists in opposition to a fixed mindset. When we have a fixed mindset, we tend to believe:

» Someone is either good at a task or not.

» Skills and abilities are internal and static.

» There is little room for personal change.

» If something is too difficult, you should just give up.

» I/That student can't do _____.

A growth mindset allows us to reframe:

» I/This student can learn new skills.

» I/He can't do _____ YET.

---

81   Carol S. Dweck, *Mindset: The New Psychology of Success* (New York: Ballantine Books, 2007).

» If you persist at a difficult task, you can learn new skills.

» Everyone can learn new things and make personal changes or improvements.

Approaching situations with a growth mindset serves two important purposes. First, students often rise or fall to your expectations of them. Even when you do not explicitly state your expectations of others, your beliefs impact all of the subtle and explicit ways you treat that person. These behavioral patterns will shape the student's behavior in one direction or the other. You might as well use that power to your advantage and truly believe your students can meet high expectations.

Second, keeping a growth mindset is a huge buffer against compassion fatigue. When you start to drift toward a fixed mindset, you begin to believe that students and their families are static beings who are either broken or healthy. You then lose hope for students and families to make progress, and in turn, begin to feel less personally and professionally effective. Try to get to a place where you can reflect on student behaviors and truly believe these behaviors can change.

GROWTH MINDSET EXERCISE

List 1 to 3 things that you used to believe but you no longer believe.

E.g., I used to believe that Santa and his reindeer brought all of my Christmas toys each year. I now understand my parents were completing these tasks.

1. _____

_____

2. _____

_____

3. _____

_____

List 1 to 3 things that you once couldn't do but can now.

E.g., I did not know how to join a virtual meeting, but now I can join and host them.

1. _____

2. _____

3. _____

When you reflect on your own growth, it's obvious that humans are capable of so much change and progress. Think about sharing these insights with your students, or even having them create their own lists, to model for them that people can always learn new information and new skills. You often feel the most hopeless about yourself and others when you are stuck in a fixed mindset.

BEHAVIORAL PATTERNS AS A SURVIVAL RESPONSE

The behaviors you see from some trauma-exposed students may seem irrational and overreactive to others in the environment. It is important to keep in mind that when a student is triggered, the reactions may be largely organic and mostly out of the student's control, originating in the limbic system or even the brain stem.

As we've previously outlined, many students respond to trauma with an "acting out" response, such as talking back to teachers, saying no, or leaving the assigned area. These reactions would be consistent with a fight-or-flight response. On the other hand, there are individuals who tend to freeze or dissociate in response to traumatic events. These students may appear quiet and passive, almost to a fault. The child who acts out with disruptive behaviors will definitely get a response and attention within the school environment.

Whether the child is lashing out or spacing out, keep in mind these behaviors are most likely not intentional or even remotely planned. Your students are not sitting at home plotting ways to ruin your day tomorrow. They are just trying to survive each of their environments and navigate relationships using their current skills based on previous experiences. We will offer strategies in a later section to respond to observed problem behaviors.

CONSIDER IF BASIC NEEDS OF STUDENT HAVE BEEN MET

In the past, psychologists and other mental health professionals believed patients could only move past the trauma they experienced if they were able to talk through and process the experience. More recently, professionals have realized the importance of meeting the individual's basic needs as part of treatment. Without adequate sleep, food, affection, or medical treatment, the chances of having psychological difficulties increases. If any of these needs are unmet, a student will not be able to stay focused and retain academic information.

As we've previously discussed, until the student feels safe, they operate from the brain stem. Until they feel connected, their behaviors will largely be a reaction of the limbic system. If you are able to help them meet their basic needs, it allows them a better chance of operating out of their rational brain.

FUNCTIONAL THINKING

Functional thinking involves understanding the function, or the "why" of problem behaviors. One of the quickest ways to consider the function is to ask yourself, "What need is this behavior meeting for this child?" This may seem simple on the surface, but determining the answer is complex and a struggle even for many veteran educators and others who support students with trauma histories.

The most important reason to consider function is to address repeated or persistent behavioral problems. When you intervene in ways that match the why of problem behaviors, problem behaviors are much more likely to decrease and desired behaviors that you expect from same-aged peers to increase. On a related note, and to address an issue that keeps us up at night, if you respond to problem behaviors with an intervention that is counter to the function, or that accidentally reinforces the problem behavior, you are likely to make the problem behavior worse and the pattern of the problem behavior more deeply ingrained. For example, if a student finds escaping academic tasks or the school environment valuable and that student is suspended for a misbehavior, you run the risk of seeing more of that same misbehavior in the future.

Another important piece to understanding functional thinking circles back to empathy and understanding. When you can view problem behaviors as how students have learned to meet their needs, you take that behavior less personally and can have empathy for the experiences in that student's learning history. This leads us to a major point about behavior: It is learned. When we understand functional thinking, we have a chance to alter that learning history moving forward. We can stop letting problem behaviors work or pay off; we call this extinction. If you do this, however, you need to ensure that you are prepared to teach a functionally equivalent replacement behavior (a better alternative that pays off the same way as the problem behavior) and to ensure that this replacement behavior works well in the school environment.

This leads us to another point related to behavior: It varies by setting and people present. Your students are likely to bring behaviors into the school environment that work for them in other settings and contexts. If you are thoughtful and proactive, you can have some influence over what behaviors work well in your environments.

To start thinking functionally, consider two main functions. Start by questioning if a student's behavior is functioning to access or obtain something desirable or if the behavior is functioning to escape or avoid something undesired or unpleasant in the environment. Next, get more detailed about *what* is being accessed or avoided. Research-based functions of behavior include adult attention, peer attention, tangible items (e.g., toy or snack), activities, and sensory stimulation (e.g., movement or noise).

Let's explore a couple examples of thinking functionally. Consider the student who hits during play or free time. Without knowing anything more about the student's behavior, start to think about what function this behavior might serve. If there was a pattern or history here where adults respond by giving attention to the student who hit, by reprimanding, redirecting, prompting another activity with the adult, or simply giving a big reaction, accessing adult attention could be the function. If there was a pattern or history of the peer dropping a toy or leaving an activity, the student's behavior could function to access the toy or activity. If the peer were to yell and have a big reaction, the function could be to access peer attention or even sensory stimulation if the peer's reaction were somehow a pleasing sight or sound.

To switch gears and think about what a student might be escaping or avoiding with the hitting behavior in this example, the behavior could function to escape peer attention if that peer then leaves the immediate environment or if an adult moves that peer away. Some of our students use aggression or intimidation to keep peers or adults out of their space or to avoid interactions. In this example, there could be characteristics about specific peers, adults, or environments that are aversive, and the hitting behavior could function to get the student away from undesirable sensory experiences. Be particularly watchful for this when supporting students with a trauma history, as sensory experiences tied to their trauma could be present in the classroom environment. Consider if an adult or student in the educational environment looks, sounds, or even smells like someone aversive in the student's history.

Another common problem behavior in the school environment that can have multiple functions is running or eloping. Starting with our broad categories, students may run from the classroom or other environment not just to escape or avoid, but also to access or obtain. A memorable student from many years ago who had a significant trauma history started to run from classrooms soon after joining a new school. Initially, the team supporting him believed that he was escaping something in the classroom and started looking for patterns; did it occur during certain academic tasks or parts of the day, or only in certain environments? The team could not find any obvious pattern and decided to complete a Functional Behavior Assessment (FBA). An FBA is a process for determining the function, or "why," of problem behavior and leads to a Behavior Intervention Plan (BIP) that addresses modifying triggers, teaching replacement behavior, reducing problem behavior, and reinforcing desired behavior.

During the FBA process, which typically involves interviews and direct observation, the team determined the student would typically run when there was minimal staff attention in the classroom due to a low staff-to-student ratio, or when staff was busy with other students. After the student left the classroom, he had a pattern of staying close by and actually waiting for whichever adult was supervising him at the time. If staff did not approach him at these times, he would then try to engage staff. The student was not trying to escape by running but rather had developed a pattern of accessing adult attention by running.

Once we understood this pattern, we were able to help this student meet his needs with a functionally equivalent replacement behavior. We taught this student to ask an adult for a break. Initially, we honored this request as soon as possible, giving adult attention and supervision during the break, and later began to introduce a delay or a work contingency (e.g., writing two more sentences) before the break time.

To be clear about a few things when you start to analyze challenging behavior:

1. The function, or why, of behavior can only reliably be determined when you see repeated patterns. You might have some idea of what needs are being met with one-off instances of behavior, but you cannot be sure what maintains patterns of behavior unless you can observe it or others can reliably report observing it happen repeatedly.

2. Part of observing behavior, to help determine function, is watching for antecedents, or fast triggers. These are whatever events happen immediately before the challenging behavior. In the above examples, the fast trigger for hitting might be that a peer picks up a preferred toy. The trigger for running might be that the teacher turned their attention to other students.

3. In addition to the antecedent or fast triggers, you need to look at the consequences or whatever happens immediately after the behavior. In the above examples, if the peer drops the preferred toy and our student gets a hold of it, that is a piece of evidence that accessing a preferred item was the function of the hitting behavior. In our other example, if after running, an adult follows and engages with our student, it is a piece of evidence that running functions to access adult attention. The more consistently you observe these patterns, the more confidence you can have in determining the needs that your students are meeting with their challenging behavior.

INTERMITTENT REINFORCEMENT

It is important to note that behaviors can be reinforced and become very well ingrained, even when they only *sometimes* work or pay off for the individual. A technical term for this is intermittent reinforcement. When behaviors are intermittently reinforced, meaning they sometimes work for the individual, they become hard to extinguish. A common example of this in adults relates to gambling. Slot machines provide a type of intermittent reinforcement. *Sometimes* there is a pay-off for the behavior of plunking a coin into the machine. The gambling industry has deep expertise in this type of human behavior, and they know the rate and magnitude of reinforcement to keep lots of people sitting at the machines for long periods of time.

The lesson you can take from the power of intermittent reinforcement is to be consistent, remembering you are human and not perfect, in not letting challenging behavior pay off. Alternatively, when you teach a new, more appropriate behavior to get a need met, make sure that behavior works very well, especially to start. If the new behavior, does not work efficiently, it is likely that your students will fall back to old behaviors, even if they only sometimes worked. For other desired behaviors, or after new behaviors have become ingrained, make sure to acknowledge or reinforce them sometimes, or intermittently, to ensure they continue.

TEACH AND PRACTICE SCHOOL-SPECIFIC BEHAVIORS

Behavior varies by environment and is specific to the context in which it occurs. It's possible that what you perceive as an inappropriate behavioral pattern at school is helping the child survive outside of school. If a student is physically fighting with other children, we can help them learn more appropriate behaviors within the school setting; however, they may need to keep their capacity to fight for survival at home and in the neighborhood.

In these situations, be mindful of your approach, coaching, "At school, we do things this way..." Even very young students are capable of learning how to code-switch or change their behaviors to match their current environment. Teach and practice school-specific behaviors.

The fact that behavior varies by environment is cause for hope. Remember that we get to have some control over the classroom and school environment. If you do not allow a problem behavior to work well at school and you teach and reinforce a school-appropriate alternative, you can help students "un-learn" some of the maladaptive patterns they may have brought with them originally.

One more note about how we and our students have learned behaviors, both desired and undesired, is that we have done so unconsciously for the most part. We have learned them through repeated associations and we engage in many behaviors without planning or conscious thought. The student who may hit to get a desired toy is not likely planning this action for play time, but is almost surely just reacting in the moment. The student who runs is not likely planning and waiting for low adult attention conditions to make a break for it, but is only reacting to the environmental conditions. While we sometimes do plan out some of our behaviors, I doubt we walk up to a store counter thinking we will smile at the cashier because it is likely we will get reinforced with the attention of getting a smile back. We are likely operating at a subconscious level and adjusting to our environment and our own learning history. Our students are doing the same thing and we can be sympathetic to their learning histories, especially if trauma is part of their experience.

REFRAMING PROBLEM BEHAVIOR AND REINFORCING THE OPPOSITE

A veteran teacher we know shared a wonderful technique with us that we want to share with you. This teacher, in attempting to know herself well, takes time to think about the problem behaviors she sees in her class, especially the ones that she finds annoying. Breaks from school are a good time for this, or perhaps after you have taken care of yourself. Once she has identified the problem behaviors that are troubling or annoying, she reframes them to their opposite in positively stated terms. For example, if talking out is a problem, then working quietly and raising your hand would be the opposite of that problem behavior. For students who may be rude or disrespectful, then kind words or being polite might be the positive reframing of disrespect.

Next comes the magic—actively looking for students displaying those positively reframed behaviors and acknowledging them. You do not even have to always direct this to the students who typically display the problem behavior, although please do studiously look for those students doing the right thing. There can be a bit of a contagion effect when you focus on noticing and acknowledging appropriate behavior. Simply put, you get more of what you acknowledge, and this applies to your class as a whole.

When you do this on a consistent basis, a few things will likely happen. For one, your perception of your students, your classroom, and your school environment will likely shift. In doing school-wide behavior work, when educators start looking to acknowledge students doing the right thing, they simply feel better about being at work. Second, your students will start showing you those positively stated expectations. Every time you acknowledge them, you are signaling to your students how to appropriately get your attention and every acknowledgement serves as a class-wide prompt.

1. List two to three minor problem behaviors (e.g., talking out or taking long to get started):

2. Reframe the problem behaviors into positively stated terms (e.g., working quietly or getting started quickly):

3. Now it is time to harness the power of adult attention (you get more of what you give attention to) by acknowledging the reframed behaviors. Remember to frequently acknowledge the more desirable behaviors at first before fading to occasional praise (e.g., Eddie, thank you for working quietly, or please give yourself a point for getting started quickly). List your plan or positive reinforcement system for letting students know they are doing the right thing.

CHAPTER 7

CREATE A **SAFE** AND **SUPPORTIVE** **ENVIRONMENT**

Creating a safe and supportive physical environment that is conducive to learning is a goal for teachers everywhere. With a better understanding of the impacts of trauma, self-care, and basic behavioral principles, you can proactively design your classroom to better foster safety and connection. With an intentional classroom layout, you can save time, effort, and headaches later on in the school year.

In this section, we recommend ways to consider staff and peer safety along with the safety of your learners with significant needs. We also recommend approaching the physical environment with an eye toward building a supportive culture where ALL students can get their needs met without resorting to the use of disruptive behavior that causes you to pause instruction. In this way, you can create a more trauma-sensitive classroom, which may help students expand their windows of tolerance.

PHYSICAL CLASSROOM LAYOUT

ALLOW FOR EASY FLOW OF STAFF AND STUDENTS

It is important to be proactive in the way you use your instructional space, especially if that space is not ideal in size or layout. Some schools struggle with overcrowded classes and outdated buildings, and in these cases, it is even more important to be thoughtful about classroom layout. One important consideration is to ensure that teachers and other adults are able to move efficiently around the room. This allows you to prevent problems by frequently circulating among your students. Students are more likely to stay on task when the teacher circulates, especially in an unpredictable pattern. This allows you to quickly get closer to students who are struggling at the moment.

Sometimes, just moving closer to students is enough to help them through moments when they are agitated. Other times, getting to them quickly to offer academic support is all they need. If a student's behavior is escalating or they are becoming agitated, using proximity to shield them from the unwanted attention of peers can be helpful.

Another consideration is to enable students to move freely. At times, you will prompt students to move to other areas of the room, and you may want to teach them to ask to move or they may learn to move independently, in order to self-regulate if they become too distracted or agitated by peers.

Whether you prefer arranging your classroom in rows of desks, seating students in small groups, or both, it is paramount for you and your students to move freely and safely around the room. Consider the developmental level of your students and your preferred instructional delivery methods. Will you want a space for circle or carpet time with your younger students? Will you want space to facilitate restorative circles or class councils? How will your space incorporate these methods of instructional delivery while accommodating movement around the room? One solution that's shown great success in smaller spaces is to teach students to rearrange the room, moving their desks from rows to groups. This allows for multiple instructional delivery methods within limited space and can be an opportunity to teach students how to work together.

Often, our best-laid plans do not pan out. You may need to rearrange your room to meet the needs of your students once you get to know them. One teacher of students on the autism spectrum, a population that generally needs well-defined spaces in the classroom, had to rearrange her classroom multiple times in the fall before settling into a space that worked for the spring. We often need to adjust to meet the needs of our learners.

AVOID CHOKE POINTS

To avoid a choke point and promote an easy classroom flow, you want to prevent having too many students funnel through any one area at the same time. This is of particular interest for students who may have trauma histories. From our experience, many children may have difficulties when they come into close contact with others, but for some students, being touched or stuck in a crowded place is a particular trigger. These students, as well as younger or more impulsive students, may show emotional reactions or physically act out when they come into incidental contact with peers.

Choke points in the classroom include:

» Areas with preferred items like computers, tablets, or other materials like crayons or markers

» Tight spaces for lining up, especially those without firm routines

» The pencil sharpener

» The water fountain

» The sink

If you work within tight spaces or with student populations that struggle with impulsivity, consider routines to direct and dismiss students by rows or groups. Another proactive example is to assign one student of a group or row to get materials or collect papers. For desired items like laptops, assigning specific devices to individuals can help prevent conflict. Using individual greetings (see Chapter 8 for further detail) can help slow down entry into the classroom if there is a choke point for hanging up backpacks and jackets inside the doorway.

Are there any parts that don't allow for easy flow? Are there any routines during which you observe a choke point where kids are bumping or crowding into each other? How might you adjust these areas or transitions?

ALLOW FOR GOOD SIGHT LINES

As you're considering easy flow and avoiding choke points, also ensure that you have good sight lines for all areas of your classroom. Simply put, as possible, set up your instructional space so that all parts of the classroom can be seen from all other parts of the classroom. This allows for frequent scanning to prevent concerns from developing or to notice and respond to student-to-student difficulties or other instances of agitation.

Good sight lines allow you to frequently visually scan the instructional setting (we will cover this in more detail in Active Supervision, page 136). This allows you to identify students who need support and to intervene early should problems begin to develop. We have had the unfortunate experience of consulting in rooms where students with significant needs were allowed to be in parts of the room behind bookcases or other barriers that were not easily supervised by visual scanning. Some of those students were involved in inappropriate actions in those spaces, and one of the first efforts to improve practices in those rooms was to rearrange furniture to allow for visual supervision. If you find yourself in unusual room setups that make visual scanning difficult, please consider creating some space boundaries and circulating the room more frequently.

USE SPACE BOUNDARIES

The use of space boundaries is another technique used with success across a wide range of ages, abilities, and needs. Those with experience in settings designed for students with autism spectrum needs have surely seen some level of space boundary use.

Space boundaries are visual cues to help students learn to understand and respect personal space and remain on task in the assigned area. Often, colored tape or room dividers are used to separate areas of the room for certain tasks. You may see areas marked off to show students where their desk needs to stay. For younger students who have trouble staying in their space or keeping their hands to themselves, you might use space boundaries at carpet or circle time. Tape boundaries can be used here as well, and some classroom rugs have squares for individual students already embedded. Teachers sometimes use bathmats or carpet samples to designate space for individual students in need.

As opposed to space boundaries that prompt students where to stay or what activities occur in particular spaces, you can also use space boundaries to show students where not to go. Teachers sometimes have difficulties with students accessing their desks, interfering with technology, etc. We have seen great success with creating teacher-only space boundaries. These might mark off a teacher's desk or the technology cart holding their laptop and document camera. It will be very important to teach this space boundary to students and be consistent in enforcing the expectation. You may want to have a very clear and pre-taught minor consequence in your classroom management system to address individual students who enter these prohibited spaces without your permission.

CREATE A DESIGNATED SAFE SPACE

An important support, especially for students with trauma histories, is to create a designated "safe space" in the classroom. A safe space can help students who get into the flight, fight, or freeze state to have an appropriate way to escape. Even at lower levels of escalation or agitation, a safe space can allow students to start self-regulating by giving them an option to access needed time and space. The hope is that by learning to take a break from triggers or an overwhelming environment, students can expand their window of tolerance.

The safe space should be inviting and comfortable and out of the sight lines of peers during their typical instructional activities. Just as with every other part of the classroom, it should be in view of the teacher at all times. The space should also be age appropriate. For younger students, a soft, carpeted area with pillows or a bean bag works well. For older students, a soft chair, a study carrel, or just a desk in the back of the room may be best.

Sometimes you need to be creative with the space in your classrooms. Other times, for older students, the safe space may need to be out of the classroom. If you have non-classroom staff like counselors or social workers, arrangements can be made for the safe space to be elsewhere. This may allow your students to build relationships with additional adults. One librarian we worked with excelled at relationship building, and her media center contained a safe space that supported many students over the years.

Just as important as creating a safe space is the need to develop and teach expectations and procedures for using it. This can get tricky as you want students to use it when they need it, but not to overuse it as an escape. We rarely see the safe space being overused, although we want to mention this as a potential pitfall. If you believe a student is overusing the safe space, consider taking some data. Record how many times per day, which parts of the day, or which activities a student is using the safe space. You may be able to find patterns that are helpful. A student may become triggered due to something in the environment or because of a particular task or activity, which may present difficulties in frustration tolerance (events outside their window of tolerance). If you find any patterns, you can begin to address them proactively. Using the data, you may also be able to find a baseline, and in time, look to limit the number of times a student is using the safe space per day.

If you suspect that a student is escaping work tasks by using the safe space, you can consider keeping the work tasks in place to be completed later to limit the value of that escape. For other students, you may begin to offer positive reinforcement for using the space only within a limited number of times per day. We would advise letting new students use the safe space at will in the beginning. This may lessen naturally as your student becomes more comfortable and builds stronger relationships and connections with others. One thing to remember: It is a better alternative for students to withdraw to the safe space than to resort to other behaviors, like tantrums or physical aggression, to get their needs met. It is also safer for a student to use the safe space as an escape than to run from the classroom or school.

Routines for accessing the safe space can vary to suit the needs of your students. For example, students can signal the need for the safe space. We suggest a non-verbal signal, such as holding up a number of fingers. Alternatively, you can allow students to move to that space independently as long as it is unoccupied. Some teachers will prompt students with the choice of using the safe space, although we strongly recommend against coercively directing students to the safe space. That is considered a time-out and is a very different procedure. The safe space is not intended for use as a consequence for misbehavior.

If you do present using the safe space as a choice, we recommend that you withdraw your attention and give your student time to process while making that choice. Standing over the student, staying in their space, or even keeping your glare and attention on them can be triggering or cause behavioral escalation. Imagine if you were emotionally escalated and someone of authority gave you a choice and then forced you to choose while they stayed in your space or continued to stare at you. Many of us would be anxious or not react well, potentially demonstrating more escalated or disruptive behaviors.

Once you have decided on your procedures for accessing the safe space, explain them to your whole class with rationale. It is important that students understand why the safe space may be needed and how to react if a peer needs to use it. Teach your students that they can help their friends by keeping any comments to themselves and continuing to focus on learning instead of staring or talking about their friend while they are in the safe space. You can teach them to welcome their friend back and offer help with the activity at hand. In our experience, students are naturally empathetic, often seemingly more so than us adults, and they will generally be sensitive to each other if we show them the way.

The safe space can be used by all students in class or just those in need. If an individual student needs to practice, it may be best for them to do so without peers present. This will also give you some time to build your relationship, connect with your student, learn more about their triggers, engage in preferred calming activities, and/or devise a covert signal for them to let you know they need the safe space.

It is best to teach and practice use of the safe space when students are calm. You may need to reteach the procedures for accessing the safe space at times;

remembering procedures when frustrated can be difficult. Your whole class may need a refresher on procedures after breaks or if the safe space becomes misused by a number of students.

It is often recommended that an adult join very young students and students with cognitive or communication delays in the safe space. This is not always possible in understaffed classrooms, but it is ideal at least for the first few times. Students at these lower ability levels do not yet have the skills to independently choose a calming strategy or remember why they are sitting in the safe space. Consider our previous discussion on co-regulation and the impact you can have if you are able to lend your calm to a student in this situation by modeling a breathing strategy or sitting calmly with them. By remaining calm and regulated, we help students become regulated more quickly.

Lastly, although we have been using the term "safe space," please consider a more developmentally appropriate name for this area. Think creatively about what will build a supportive culture and also fit your classroom's style. Examples could include the Calm Corner, the Chill Zone, the Break Spot, or anything else that conveys a safe and calming place.

SAFE SPACE EXERCISE

Think about your students and their need to escape or take a break. Do you have a designated area in your classroom or school environment for students to access as a safe space? If not, what might work for you and your students?

CREATE CLEARLY DEFINED WORK SPACES

Having clearly designated work spaces may be an important technique, depending on your student population and their needs. Some students struggle to differentiate between play and work spaces, and you may need to keep play, free time, or break areas separate from their work spaces. If you expect students to move between work and non-academic spaces, it will be important to teach these routines and expectations proactively and then be consistent in redirecting students to these expectations.

Rules and expectations for each of these areas will likely be important. For example, think about how teachers of young children might teach different expectations for behavior at a desk (e.g., sit up with four on the floor, have your pencil ready, and look to the teacher when they are talking) as opposed to circle time (e.g., sit crisscross applesauce, keep hands and feet to yourself) or even play time (e.g., use nice hands and feet, let others play, share your materials, listen for the teacher to give instructions). Please remember that students, especially those with a history of trauma, may need clear expectations of what to do in different spaces and environments.

POST EXPECTATIONS OR RULES

It is very important to post expectations prominently in the classroom. Post them where your instruction is most often delivered, as this allows for efficiently reviewing the expectations and for nonverbal redirection; you can simply point to the expectations when you have a student's attention. Posted expectations can help adults as well. It can help you remember to use those expectations as cues or prompts and give confidence to students by pointing out when they are doing the correct things in the classroom.

The discipline of Positive Behavioral Interventions and Supports (PBIS) helps inform us about the nature of effective rules or expectations (www.pbis.org). PBIS highlights the importance of stating your expectations positively and of differentiating them from traditional rules. Rules typically tell students what not to do. The problem with this is that we assume students know what is expected and when to do what is expected. Too often, students do not know the expectations or have not generalized them to all school environments.

In addition, when you punish students for breaking the rules, you often only suppress behavior. When this occurs without a system to teach what is expected, you often do not see the behavioral change you want, especially when punishment is continued or amplified. Instead, you may see other problem behaviors begin to emerge. This is a particular concern for students at risk for emotional or behavioral difficulties and students who have been exposed to trauma. Some examples of positively stated behavioral expectations instead of rules include: "walking feet" instead of "no running," "quiet voices" instead of "no shouting," "safe hands" instead of "no hitting," etc. Are there any rules at your school or in your classroom that can be reframed as positively stated expectations?

If possible, link classroom expectations to school-wide expectations. Ideally, they will be the same. It is good practice to have three to five positively stated expectations that always apply (e.g., Be Safe, Show Respect, or Choose Responsibility). Schools with PBIS frameworks take this a step further and implement a matrix that breaks down broad school-wide expectations into specific behaviors by area of the school. For example, safety in the classroom might include students keeping all four legs of their chair on the floor or signing out when leaving the room. Safety in the cafeteria may include students washing their hands or listening to the adults. Using walking feet might be a safe expectation for all areas of the school, repeated across the matrix, perhaps with the exception of the playground or gym.

While we know that having the same broad positively stated expectations in place across all school settings is good practice, not all schools are there yet. In the absence of school-wide expectations, teachers can define these for their classrooms. This can often build classroom culture and lead to students feeling safe and connected. Some classrooms or programs develop their own expectations (e.g., Show respect by following directions quickly). Some teachers have had success with defining broad positively stated expectations and then having students brainstorm the specific behaviors that meet each expectation. In general, when teaching behavioral expectations, it is good practice to review or discuss examples and non-examples (e.g., demonstrating safe seating with four on the floor then demonstrating an example of unsafe seating with the chair tilted back). A word of caution regarding having students model or practice any of the non-examples. It is fine if adults model the non-examples, but for students, doing so can accidentally reinforce doing the wrong thing. It is better if they can receive acknowledgement or reinforcement for displaying behavior that meets expectations.

One of the reasons that we post positively stated expectations along with teaching them to our students (covered in Chapter 7) is to redirect or cue students with positively stated language. It can be a big shift for adults to start using positively stated language to correct problem behavior. Most of us are used to using "stop," "no," and "don't." There are cultural reasons for this, and these responses to problem behavior do tend to work in the moment, but not as effectively in the long term. We often fall into a sort of behavioral trap. For many problem behaviors, just giving the adult attention of a reprimand can accidentally reinforce the behavior in the long term and also signal to peers how to get attention. For example, when a teacher reprimands a student for talking out, typically that student will stop talking out in the moment. The problem is that the student also got attention, and if adult attention is valuable to that student, they may soon talk out again. We know that this can spread to other peers. Repeated reprimands to peers for talking out (e.g., saying, "Johnny, stop talking") can serve as a cue for students who were quiet to start talking out. Please remember that we often fall into this behavioral trap because, in the moment, the problem behavior has stopped.

So, what are you to do? One method for low-level problem behaviors is to redirect with positively stated expectations and use proximity reinforcement. Instead of saying "Stop talking," you can redirect with "Work quietly, please." You can take this a step further and limit any attention to the misbehaving student by noticing and acknowledging peers who are meeting expectations. If Johnny is talking and you see Susie working quietly, you can simply say, "Susie is doing a great job working quietly." Often this subtle cue is enough for Johnny to correct his behavior, and it signals to peers how to appropriately get the teacher's attention. When you do this regularly, you are consistently reminding your students of the expectations. Again, posting your expectations is a great way to prompt yourself and other adults to use this language effectively. For your students who have experienced trauma and adversity, this direct and positive approach will feel more safe than reactive behavioral strategies. A predictable set of expectations can lead to a safer environment and an expanded window of tolerance.

POST AND REVIEW DAILY SCHEDULE

Students and adults alike benefit from consistency and predictability. This is especially true for students at risk for emotional and behavioral concerns, students with autism spectrum needs, and students who have been exposed to trauma. You may be able to connect to your experience of plans changing, not knowing what is coming next, or knowing what to expect from people in authority; uncertainty can cause or worsen anxiety. Predictability and consistency can be a universal support for everyone and a way to foster feelings of safety and connectedness for students with a history of trauma. We acknowledge that you cannot have complete control over all the factors in a school environment, but you can foster this sense of stability as much as possible.

It is a good practice to list the schedule for the day prominently in the classroom, such as on the board or near your instructional space. It is even better to review the schedule as part of the routine to start the school day. For younger learners, the schedule may consist of a series of pictures that correspond to daily activities. As noted, changes will happen. You cannot account for the fire alarm going off, other teachers being out sick, or the internet to stop working right before that great lesson you had planned. What you can do is let your students know when those unexpected changes do occur, and then update your schedule. Some students will become overly focused and concerned if exact times listed on the schedule are not closely followed. For example, if math practice after a lesson is going really well, some teachers will stick with that subject and maybe cut another subject short. If you have students who are overly concerned with timing, you can always leave the times off of an academic block and just note the times for things that will not change, like lunch and dismissal.

Some students may protest if they see something they do not like on the schedule. It is our opinion and experience that it is generally best to address those concerns at the beginning of the day rather than in the moment when it is time to transition to that undesired activity. Some teachers use a symbol or picture, such as a star, on the schedule when there will be a special activity, indicating a change in the schedule.

One other consideration related to things not always going as planned is to have some engaging backup activities always on hand. You may be in a position where your technology needed for a lesson stops working or you need to leave the room for a room clear procedure. It is a good idea to have something portable and engaging for your students at the ready. This could be a passive activity like reading a book to the class or having paper and pencil tasks like word searches ready to go. Anything that you could pull off the shelf and that your students are familiar with and interested in will work. This would not be the time for a novel task, so if it is a paper and pencil activity, be sure you have taught your students the routine for the activity ahead of time.

POST VISUAL PROMPTS AND ROUTINES

Visual prompts are a particularly important support for students with developmental delays and those who are in the process of language acquisition. In the context of a safe and supportive environment, these are often posted on the walls for all to see or in specific areas where they apply, such as handwashing prompts over the sink. To help with transitioning out of the classroom, you may post the steps to lining up, a picture of students lined up correctly, or pictures of feet with appropriate spacing near the door. You can also include prompts on desks or tables that apply to all students, like a number line for younger children or reminders of hand raising or the safe space request signal for individual students.

Visual prompts give students the signposts they need to operate with more independence in the classroom. Fostering independence has the potential to increase resilience. In general, consider posting anything that your students may need to reference frequently as an academic support. Consider posting pictorial representations of any common routines and frequent prompts or redirections you may need.

Common academic support prompts vary with age and developmental level. For elementary school students, consider items like the alphabet, the number line, math symbols, and their name on their desk. Think about how you can foster independence and lessen the need for students to ask you or others for routine information. For older students, you may want to post examples on the walls of equations or the parts of speech after you teach them. We have seen talented math teachers post example math equations that build off each other sequentially along the walls of the classroom to facilitate quick review and reference. This is particularly helpful in school environments where students struggle with absenteeism. Students can quietly review the information displayed in the classroom without added attention to their absence or missed instruction.

Explicitly teaching and practicing classroom and school routines and procedures is another universal support that also can greatly benefit our special populations. While positively stated expectations should always apply, routines and procedures are what we want students to do in context (in certain situations or at certain times). Common routines can include how to get assistance, how to gain permission to leave for the bathroom, how to access materials, how to enter the classroom appropriately, and how to line up when leaving. You may wish to teach a set of routines and procedures at the beginning of the year based on what you anticipate your students will need. Then, add additional routines as your students let you know they need the support of more explicit procedures. Post the steps for procedures close to where they will be practiced to help cut down on teaching and reteaching time. Students can reference them when reminders are needed, and you can use nonverbal prompting, such as pointing or gesturing to the prompts. Consider using pictures when possible, with or without corresponding text.

Picture prompts can be especially helpful if students are frustrated or agitated. Recall our discussion on the loss of language in Chapter 2. All humans begin to lose the ability to process language and understand verbal information when they are triggered or anxious. Students with trauma histories may experience this loss of language processing even more quickly than typically developing students, as they will likely be triggered outside their smaller window of tolerance more easily. Many teachers have success using photos of students displaying the desired steps in routines. This can be a helpful practice, but be sure to adhere to any policies or needed permissions before photographing students.

SET CLEAR PROCEDURES TO ACCESS MATERIALS

Many educators overlook the need to create set procedures for what materials students can access and how. You will likely also want to determine what materials are only to be accessed with an adult. We will address items that may be dangerous later, but here we want to focus on more common classroom materials and also circle back to ensuring there is adequate space for the flow of students and staff to avoid choke points. The developmental level and any special needs of your students are again considerations to keep in mind as you think about what materials students can access independently. You can give students free access or have them use a simple hand signal for items like paper and pencils. Other items, like scissors, calculators, lab equipment, or art supplies, may only be accessible by adults. You can always assign specific students to pass out these items.

For items that are in high demand, like tablets or laptops, have them distributed by an adult or set procedures for students to access them in an orderly manner. A rush for highly desirable items, especially near a choke point, can bring students into close proximity. This can lead to pushing, shoving, or more intense physical altercations. This also has the potential to trigger emotional reactions in your more vulnerable students. You may want to consider numbering and assigning these items so that students have a sense of ownership. This can foster responsibility and also provide an easy means of directing students to access those items in a more orderly fashion (e.g., If your tablet is numbered 1 through 5, please retrieve your device now).

Consider designating a secure place for adults to store students' items under lock and key. This can be important for some student populations that may impulsively pocket the items of others. Students who experience food insecurity or other similar challenges may have difficulties keeping themselves away from the possessions of others. Students who have experienced significant trauma and adversity are often living in survival mode and may witness theft outside of school. They might not even realize the impact of stealing or taking the possessions of others. If you have teacher assistants or volunteers, it can be a support for them to have secure storage for personal items in the classroom. Lastly, students may bring items to school that, while not dangerous, are inappropriate and need to be locked up.

We have vivid memories of students who live in group homes or who are homeless bringing important possessions to school. In one instance, a high school student brought her tablet to school and a staff member took it from her with little sensitivity. That student's reactions quickly moved from emotional (limbic system) to physically aggressive (brain stem), and it was a dangerous moment for all involved. Fortunately, this student had good advocates at school, and we learned that the tablet was the only mode of communication and connection she had with her last known family member. The item was not safe to be left unattended at her group home. We were able to support that student by creating a locked safe space for her items and a depersonalized system for her to store and retrieve them. This support built trust and provided some small measure of security that helped the student to flourish in time.

ACCESSING MATERIALS

List the materials/items students can access independently and where they will be stored. List the materials/items only adults can access and where those items can be stored:

Student Materials   **Storage Location**

_____   _____

_____   _____

_____   _____

_____   _____

_____   _____

Adult Materials   **Storage Location**

_____   _____

_____   _____

_____   _____

_____   _____

_____   _____

LIMIT CLUTTER AND VISUAL OVERSTIMULATION

Clean and orderly educational environments can be helpful to students in a number of ways. Too much clutter can be distracting, especially to students with attention difficulties or those with difficulties focusing for any number of reasons. As we discussed in Chapter 3, students with a history of trauma may already struggle to complete tasks and remain focused. These students can be overly sensitive to visual stimuli in their environment and demonstrate hypervigilance that distracts from important classroom work.

Clutter or excess materials can also be a barrier to the free-flowing movement of students and adults. While you want your classrooms and other educational environments to be visually appealing, we caution against overstimulating environments. Make space for visual prompts and representations of routines and procedures, but do not overcrowd your walls and other spaces. We appreciate and support teachers using themes that express their personality. This can build culture and connection into the classroom, but try to find a balance that leaves a sense of organization. Creative storage solutions, such as cabinets and bins for instructional materials that are not used on a frequent basis, can organize materials and minimize clutter.

USE AGE-APPROPRIATE THEMES AND DECOR

As much as possible, try to decorate your classroom and plan your lessons around age-appropriate themes. This may be more of a concern for classrooms designed for students with developmental delays, but we feel it is important to mention in context as a universal support for all students and those who may have experienced trauma.

We can appreciate that students may have varied interests and that sometimes those interests are not in line with same-age peers. Some students are still interested in activities and themes from a much younger age, while others have been exposed to adult content and are drawn toward more mature themes. You will often tap into individual interests to build motivation, but be careful to avoid infantilizing students with special needs. Some students may not have access to popular and age-appropriate toys and media content. Exposing them to more varied topics can help them foster relationships with peers.

SEAT STRATEGICALLY

Experienced teachers often seat individual students strategically within their classrooms. You can't always predict student needs until you get to know them individually, but you can do a few things to be prepared for a wide range of students in your classroom. Consider what types of instruction will be a good fit for your students: rows, small groups, carpet time, etc. We advise you to assign seats from the start and also let students know that you will be changing up seating arrangements periodically. If students need rationale, you can let them know you will sometimes move them to best get them what they need. You can also speak to the importance of establishing community and set the expectation that all students will get to learn and play together throughout the course of the year. As you build relationships with individual students (more in Chapter 8), you will be able to further build that trust and connection. When we explain to children that some peers are still working on skills like sitting, working quietly, using nice words, or getting work completed, their natural empathy takes over and they accept differences and often try to support their peers.

Even before you get to know your students, you can anticipate common needs and plan accordingly. Think about putting the student who needs a lot of attention or connection, extra prompting, and maybe that extra dose of love in a location near your main instructional space. If you typically deliver whole-group instruction from a document camera or your laptop, consider seating students in close proximity to that space. For students who are highly distractible, either due to attention-impacting disorders or the potential effects of trauma, seats and spaces where they will have fewer distractions can be helpful. Once you get to know other students' strengths, you may move your distractible student near those who are almost always on task and generally kind and helpful. Often, being seated next to such a peer works as a natural motivator to cue back to tasks.

You will likely have students with movement needs. Think about seating them where they will not distract peers to a great degree, such as in the back, where they can stand at their desk, lie on the floor, or engage in other movements that you've agreed upon. Some students will need to leave the classroom often, whether it be for toileting needs, to see the nurse, or for special education services. Consider seating them near the door so their transitions are less disruptive and perhaps less embarrassing for them. Regarding the safe space we talked about earlier, if you have a student who utilizes this space often, consider seating them within close proximity.

Some students will need their own personal space, which differs from using a safe space, as the safe space is not student specific. This individual space might be their own work space or involve something to limit distractions, like a study carrel. Some students may need to sit with peers and then a separate space to use as needed to help them regulate. Others may need a balance ball seat, a standing desk, a rocking chair, etc. Offering these types of options is sometimes referred to as flexible seating. Often, students are allowed some choice within teacher-approved parameters. At other times, the teacher may suggest these arrangements or moves temporarily. As with the use of the safe space, make sure you are not directing these seating choices as a consequence for misbehavior. Try to provide the choice as neutrally as possible to prevent escalating student behavior or triggering additional anxiety.

MANAGE DANGEROUS OBJECTS AND SUBSTANCES

To help create a safe and supportive classroom, take inventory and action with any potentially dangerous objects and substances. Some dangerous objects might be obvious, like scissors, metal-edged rulers, or protractors. Some less obvious dangerous objects might be technology devices like tablets and laptops, which can make dangerous projectiles. Other items to consider might be things that students bring in from recess, like sharp sticks and rocks. Jon, as a child, found a way to harness the sun using a large magnifying glass from the classroom into a fire hazard at recess time. Sensing Jon and his friends were up to mischievous ends with this item, their teacher soon restricted access to the magnifying glass. Children can be very creative by engaging in inappropriate play with dangerous objects and at times may use these classroom items to threaten or harm others. If you find this to be the case, restrict access to those potentially dangerous items at all times or remove them when students become escalated.

In another example, Jon was helping a high school team develop behavioral supports for a student with autism spectrum needs and a history of aggressive behavior. The team learned that this student tended to separate himself from others when he became highly escalated or frustrated. If this attempt to regulate himself was unsuccessful, physical aggression was likely to follow. The school team shared that he had recently hidden out in a closet on the high school campus. The problem was that this closet was used by Junior ROTC and housed...swords. You read that right; there was an unlocked closet containing swords and an escalated student had found that closet. Fortunately, these were swords used in drills, and they were not sharp. No one was hurt, although the potential for harm was high. The first recommendation to the school team was to lock the sword closet! After that, the team created a defined space for the student and taught him how he could remove himself to help him self-regulate moving forward.

Some dangerous substances in the classroom are also easy to overlook. Cleaning products can be dangerous to students who do not have the safety awareness to avoid playing with or investigating them. A staff member's hot coffee could become a dangerous substance if spilled or splashed. Art supplies sometimes need management, and for older grades, lab equipment most likely needs to be secured. Additionally, any substance that a student is allergic to could be a dangerous substance in the classroom.

Conducting a regular sweep of your classroom to assess any dangerous objects or substances is a good preventative practice. If an escalated student does get a hold of a dangerous item, please remember your school's crisis intervention procedures, if applicable, and, in general, look to move others to safety.

Dangerous items brought by students from home are also a concern. You certainly need to watch for students who bring weapons or drugs. We recommend teaching students what is acceptable and unacceptable at school while being clear about your local laws and policies. Those rules may differ from the cultural norms your students experience in their families or communities.

We suggest teaching your class to report any suspicious or concerning items. As you build trusting relationships with your students, they will likely be a source of information as they discover dangerous items or substances that peers have hidden. This has certainly been our experience in schools, and peer reports have prevented possible injuries and exposure to drugs or medications. We do not recommend intervening alone if you suspect students have dangerous items in their possession. Doing so can be dangerous to you and your students. Consider a room clear procedure or other elements of your school safety plan if you need to get your class to safety. Do remember that your students have rights and that school administrators are typically best trained to intervene while respecting those rights.

CREATE AN "ALL DONE" BIN OR BASKET

Designating containers to temporarily store student items that cannot be used in the classroom is a great way to create a safe and supportive space. This simple technique seems to work with a wide range of students, from preschoolers with special needs to typically developing high schoolers. We believe it works because it depersonalizes the process of giving up desired items. An "all done" basket or bin (call it whatever fits with your classroom culture and personality), for example, is a safe place for high school students to put their cell phones where phone use is prohibited. Students who are reluctant to give their phones to a staff member are often more willing to comply when the directive is to place the item into a basket. We have seen young students with developmental delays learn to give up preferred items like tablets when the procedure of using an "all done" bin was consistently used as needed for individual students or as a classroom procedure. But like other procedures, it will work better if it is taught, modeled, practiced, and reinforced.

✓CHAPTER CHECKLIST
Creating a Supportive Classroom Environment

Use this list of considerations when setting up your classroom or when you want to revisit your classroom layout and environment. We by no means want to suggest that all of these supports are necessary for all populations and settings. The checklist serves as a quick reference of general practices to refer to as needed.

❑ Allow for easy flow of staff and students.

❑ Avoid choke points.

❑ Design good sight lines.

❑ Consider the use of space boundaries.

❑ Create a safe space and teach and practice related procedures as needed.

❑ Clearly define work spaces.

❑ Post expectations or rules.

❑ Post and review daily schedules.

❑ Post and use visual prompts and routines.

❑ Set clear procedures to access materials.

❑ Limit clutter and visual overstimulation.

❑ Use themes and decor that are age appropriate.

❑ Use assigned seats that consider individual spaces and flexibility.

❑ Manage dangerous objects and substances.

❑ Maintain the use of an "all done" bin or basket.

CHAPTER 8

BUILD RELATIONSHIPS

As we move forward into proactive and reactive strategies to support student emotions and behaviors, consider that any strategies you implement will be much more effective if you have a good relationship with the student. It is almost impossible to overstate the importance of developing genuine relationships. One of the greatest predictors of a student's success is their perception of whether or not you like them. In fact, we have heard from many sources that the only thing that can truly shift a person's trajectory (besides a spiritual experience) is a genuine, connected relationship.[82]

If students have positive, healthy relationships, they can buffer their exposure to trauma and build resilience. On the flip side, if they don't have positive healthy relationships, they may demonstrate symptoms of trauma exposure even without having traumatic experiences.

A secure attachment with an early caregiver helps build an internal locus of control in children, or the sense that they can solve problems or impact their environment and its outcomes. This secure attachment also helps the child learn that

---

82 Rick Griffin, "Trauma-Supportive Certification: Course Two," Phoenix, Arizona, lecture, October 25, 2019.

intensely negative experiences will be met with care and comfort from the parent or caregiver. Students who have experienced inconsistent parenting or trauma and neglect will not have this foundation on which to build.[83] They often feel hopeless or resigned to failure, blaming the world around them.

Historically, natural experiences within a tribe, extended family, or community have helped young people develop appropriate social connections and attachments. Human patterns of living have shifted greatly, especially in Western societies. For thousands of generations we lived in small, multigenerational groups, with dramatically higher ratios of caregiver to young child. In "primitive" cultures, a child would have 100 relational experiences during the day.[84] In today's world, the average is 10 minutes of caregiver quality time each day with children, and that is usually if the family sits for a meal together or has a bedtime routine. Many of your students who live in families with chronic trauma or stress do not even receive these 10 minutes outside of school.

Students will project on to you what they've experienced with other adults through their histories of relational patterns. If they've had a secure attachment with caregivers, they will likely tolerate your social interactions and respond as you would expect. If that has not been the case, and they have experienced trauma and adversity, your interactions may violate a boundary and inadvertently trigger a threat response. It's important to remember in these moments that the student's emotional or survival response is not personal to you, and that you can help him feel safe and connected in order to shift this response.

You cannot change what has already happened in your student's life before they enter your classroom, but you can help children build resilience as they move forward. Resilience is the buffering or mitigating of the threat response and how that plays out in the student's behavior. If you can create a safe and protective relationship with a student, you can help prevent them from further long-term problems. A positive adult relationship with a child is more predictive of success than IQ, socioeconomic status, and countless other variables.[85]

---

83   van der Kolk, *The Body Keeps Score*, 115.
84   Van Parys, "Neurosequential Model."
85   van der Kolk, *The Body Keeps Score,* 162.

A key aspect of supporting a trauma-exposed child is to help them help themself. Doing too many things to solve problems for them is not helpful in the long term. Rather, it is more productive for a student to build a sense of autonomy and knowledge so they can affect the outcomes of a situation in their life.[86] Lend your guidance and support while the student learns new, more appropriate ways to meet their needs.

There are going to be student behaviors that irritate you as the educator. Each person naturally has an easier time building relationships with certain students, generally those who do not trigger their own anxiety and stress reactions. However, as the professionals in the situation, we have a responsibility to find a way to build a genuine relationship. Students can often tell whether your attention is genuine and caring, so you may need to focus some energy on finding things to legitimately enjoy about some of your students. You cannot teach a child you dislike; the intent must be genuine.

DEED VERSUS DOER

Sometimes, it may feel impossible for you to find a way to reframe problematic behaviors. Maybe you cannot fathom why a student would engage in the behaviors you observe. Recall our conversations in Chapter 6 on positive intent and functional thinking. Each student is doing the best they can with the problems and skills they have. When you build a relationship with students, you take the time to understand their problems. With this understanding, you can help them find more appropriate or healthy ways to meet their own needs.

If you are struggling to like a particular student, you may need to focus on separating the deed from the doer. The behavior is not the student, and the student is not the behavior. One of our mentors and master teachers, Debbie Voll, prompts educators to think about which behaviors in the classroom bother them the most. Then, find something about that behavior you like. As she points out, compassion and anger cannot coexist when you are considering a student behavior. Take a minute to think about a particular student or a few behaviors that really get under

---

86   van der Kolk, *The Body Keeps Score*, 344.

your skin. Consider how you can separate the deed from the doer. How can you reframe that behavior to find something you like about it?

WHAT DO I LIKE ABOUT THIS BEHAVIOR?

Think of a problematic behavior you have observed recently. Name and describe the behavior. Then think of at least one thing you can appreciate about that behavior.

Example:

Behavior
Shouting answers during instruction

What do I like?
He is eager to connect with me and share ideas.

Consider taking this a step further and remember our exercise of reframing a problem behavior. How can you reframe this problem behavior into a positively stated expectation? For example, you might say, "Anthony, I love that you want to share, so next time raise your hand. I will be watching for you."

RELATIONSHIP-BUILDING STRATEGIES

As discussed in Chapter 3, safety and connection are key to healing past traumas and building resilience against future adversity. Developing a relationship with each student can help break these cycles of trauma and adversity and help expand their window of tolerance moving forward. Keep in mind you cannot be everything to everyone. You may want to assign yourself to be the primary contact for the students who have already connected with you or maybe for the students who have not yet connected with any staff members.

Consider how you can rally other school professionals to build relationships with some of your students (administrators, coaches, aides, front office staff, counselors, psychologists, etc.). All of those "connection-seeking" behaviors that are disrupting your classroom can be turned into a positive experience if you are proactive in giving the student that connection more appropriately. Teaching a student to seek connection through appropriate relationships with safe adults will help build resilience as they get older. Remembering that you can't be the go-to person for each student will help buffer you against compassion fatigue.

Considering these above variables, we want to present you with some concrete and specific relationship-building strategies.

One of the easiest ways to begin building a relationship with a student is to find something they are interested in and talk with them about it. For example, ask the student about their favorite video game, weekend plans, or sports team. If you show genuine interest in the student's response, you start building that safety and connection through your relationship. You can do this informally as you go throughout your day, focusing on all students or particular students. Below are some more intentional and structured formats for these conversations.

CO-REGULATE TO CALM

Recall our discussion on co-regulation and how we all unintentionally match the energies of the living things in our environment. We can use this natural response to our advantage when building relationships with our students. Approach a student with care and a sense of safety and connection, and you can help expand their window of tolerance. Keep building your own calm energy so you can lend it as needed during these student interactions.

Lending calm is one of the practices we have personally experienced and observed to be highly effective. If you are in a situation with another person who becomes escalated or agitated, try to remain as calm and peaceful as possible. If they start speaking loudly or quickly, focus on using a quiet and slow voice or not responding verbally at all. After you have lent your calm to a student, they are more likely to trust you and feel safe with you. They have learned that you are a predictable and reliable adult. Relationship building should be more effective under these conditions.

TWO-BY-TENS

Think of your students who are the most disruptive, challenging, or difficult to connect with. These students might be ideal to target with a more structured relationship-building strategy like Two-by-Ten.[87] Using this strategy, you spend two minutes a day for 10 days connecting with the student by allowing them to talk to you about any preferred topic. Implementation of Two-by-Ten has led to decreased disruptive behaviors and increased school motivation and work completion.

The idea behind Two-by-Ten is to get past small talk and learn about the student outside of school. Find out about their favorite hobbies, foods, and TV shows. Keep it genuine and authentic. Try to find a good time to chat with your student while other students are engaged with work or while the class is transitioning. With older students, we've seen teachers build this time into end-of-day processing or while walking with the student during a transition such as lunch. With younger children, we've seen educators spend two minutes with the child while other students are arriving in the morning, while playing on the playground, or during a snack time.

If you can't find the time to do the full two minutes each day, at least try to spend 30 seconds talking with the student. The key here is not to spend 20 minutes talking to the student every 10 days but to build that consistent daily connection. It's better to spend even a few seconds connecting with the student each day rather than skip a week and then spend 15 minutes. Some students may appear uncomfortable or even not talk until the second week. If you make it a habit to connect with one or two of your most challenging learners each day, you will likely see positive results in your classroom and keep the momentum going after the 10 days have passed.

INDIVIDUAL GREETINGS

In order to create safety and connection, students in your classroom should have a way of honoring another's presence when greeting each other and saying goodbye to each other. If nothing else, ensure each student gets an individual, face-to-face greeting each day. Some teachers have developed secret handshakes with students or systems where a child can choose how they want to be greeted. Our

---

87   Sarah McKibben, "The Two-Minute Relationship Builder," *ASCD Education Update* 56, no. 7 (July 2014), http://www.ascd.org/publications/newsletters/education_update/jul14/vol56/num07/The_Two-Minute_Relationship_Builder.aspx.

younger students love to point to a picture to choose either hug, handshake, or high five when a teacher greets them each morning.

Along with personal daily greetings for each student in your class, make it a point to greet other students as you see them around the school environment. We like to focus extra warm attention and greetings on two particular groups of students:

New Students. If you have a student who is new to your school mid-year, they have already experienced at least one ACE in that school change. It is possible this move or school change was also precipitated by events that were not completely fun and joyful, perhaps additionally ACEs. The least we can do is greet new students warmly as they enter our school. When walking through the front office, Jon will make sure to talk to any students who are newly registered and receiving a class schedule, asking for their name, telling them we are so glad they are joining our school family, and making a positive comment about their new teacher or class. We can help these students feel a bit safer and connected on their first day.

Late Students. We sometimes see students arriving late to school and receiving a sarcastic response from office staff or teachers (e.g., "so nice of you to join us today") or receiving extra expectations in the classroom (e.g., "alright, now you need to catch up on everything you just missed"). If a student is tardy, it is unlikely that their day has gone smoothly up to that point. There was potential home conflict, stress, no breakfast, etc., and the student still made it to school. Be a reinforcer upon their arrival. Offer a warm greeting, show genuine caring that they arrived safely, and get them started on a task that can be somewhat easily completed. If you decide to approach at this moment with sarcasm or increased task demands, you may increase agitation, shrink their window of tolerance, and observe disruptive behaviors.

As an added layer of greeting, some of our teachers have incorporated greetings between peers. Each student is greeted by their teacher individually upon arrival or early in the school day. Additionally, a student in the class has a daily "job" or role of greeting their peers individually. For younger students, the child usually offers a few picture choices to peers and the peers can then verbalize or point to their preferred greeting. With older students, you could have a rotating role for peer greeter or something of the like. This role also provides structured social interactions for those students who do not have a lot of practice using prosocial skills. Older students can also be assigned or chosen as new student ambassa-dors, greeting new students as they enroll and showing them around the school. You want students to identify with the school community. If they feel as though they belong and are connected, students are more likely to be positively influenced by others in the group. Each of these greetings, whether peer-to-peer or staff-to-peer, build an increased sense of safety and connection in your environment.

PERSONALIZE YOUR GREETINGS

Think of a few ways to incorporate personal greetings into your routines or environment.

LEARN THE CULTURAL DIFFERENCES OF YOUR STUDENTS

Many classrooms and communities are becoming increasingly diverse and multi-cultural. There is a wealth of resources on creating culturally sensitive classrooms while considering racial inequities. Differences are not just evident across eth-nicity, race, or country of origin. There are also cultural differences between families of similar racial and ethnic backgrounds. Some families are louder and more energetic than others. Some are affectionate and cuddly while others expect more personal space and distance. There are also cultural differences related to religious beliefs, holiday celebrations, and dietary restrictions. Families place different levels of pressure on children for success in school and other areas of life. Get to know your students and their families as they enter your classroom. Some of our teachers use a home interest inventory or student survey to gather information about family traditions and personal expectations. Understanding the family's goals and intentions can help you build more genuine relationships with your students and their family members.

CULTURAL DIFFERENCES

Consider your current and previous students. What cultural differences are apparent? How can you gather more information from your students and families in this area?

POSITIVE FAMILY CONTACTS

Over the years, we have watched some of the most masterful teachers build pro-active relationships with the families of their most challenging learners. You can often tell within the first week which students have had negative home or classroom experiences in the past. Those kids who are disruptive, connection-seeking, and appear overreactive have probably experienced disciplinary action in previous classrooms and/or at home. Master teachers notice these red flags and get ahead of the game by calling families during the first week to share something positive about the student. Families are often caught off guard by receiving a positive message home from school. This is especially true considering we often call parents or guardians to tell them about a disruptive behavior that has already occurred and they cannot do anything to change what has already happened in the school environment. These negative family contacts may only lead to more stress and trauma in the home in the form of punishment that often doesn't improve the student's behaviors.

Researchers have started studying the impact of these positive family contacts on student behaviors. There is some literature in print on positive parent contacts, a more inclusive term of family contacts as many of our students do not live with their biological parents. Teachers are encouraged to make positive contact with the family twice per week, telling them how the student met one of the classroom or school expectations (e.g., "Julie was safe in line today by keeping her hands by her sides"). Early findings on positive family contacts have shown improved student behaviors in class and increases in reciprocal communication with the family.[88]

---

88   Liane Wardlow, "The Positive Results of Parent Communication: Teaching in a Digital Age," Pearson Education, December 2013, https://www.pearsoned.com/wp-content/uploads/DigitalAge_ ParentCommunication_121113.pdf.

You can take this to the next level by surveying family members at the beginning of the school year to ask their preferred mode of communication (email, phone call, note in the backpack, etc.). You can also ask your students if they have preferred family members they would like you to inform when they've done well. Some students care more about their grandpa or their older brother receiving positive reports.

STRIVE FOR COOPERATION

In general, classroom strategies are going to be much less effective if the student does not believe you are on their side. In the past, educators have relied on coercive methods to get students to comply with expectations or directions (e.g., "If you don't get this done, you're going to miss recess AGAIN"). Each of these coercive interactions at best takes away the student's opportunity to be independent and learn skills for next time, and at worst, re-traumatizes the student. Along with coercion, staff members also need to avoid capitulation. If you give a direction, and then change the expectation when the student's behaviors escalate, they learn that this is not a safe and predictable environment. They also learn a maladaptive way to get their needs met in the classroom and the problem behavior is potentially reinforced.

When you use one of these coercive or capitulating approaches instead of working to cooperate with your students, your relationship with the students can easily be damaged.

It's so easy to fall into one of these traps, especially as staff anxiety rises. You may feel like you need to take control of the situation and fall prey to coercive strategies. Or you start to feel like you can't manage the situation so you drop the expectations and move on (e.g. "Fine, just go to recess."). Between these two extremes, you can strive for cooperation with the student (e.g. "Let's get this done so we can go to recess."). Ally yourself with the child in order to help them meet their needs in a more appropriate way. Express that you want them to meet their goal and suggest a strategy or two choices to help them complete the task.

Strategies that help build cooperation will be covered more thoroughly in later chapters. In the meantime, consider how you can use neutral prompts to become the child's ally. When the timer goes off at the end of an interval, you can express,

"Oh! I also wish we could continue this activity, but the timer tells us it's time to get ready for math." This approach allows you to side with your students instead of creating a power struggle between you and them.

DEVELOP SILENT PROMPTS/REQUESTS

In order to build and maintain positive relationships with learners who have a decreased window of tolerance, some of our teachers have allowed the use of private cues or signals. These covert prompts allow the student to access strategies without drawing public attention to a student in need. When a student is beginning to show signs of escalation or anxiety, allow them to cue you with a hand signal or respond to a signal you give. This could be either to take a break or employ a previously taught coping strategy. For example, when you see a student start to demonstrate frustration behaviors, give them the "okay" sign with your hand so they know they can take a break and get a drink of water. If you can help them save face and calm down without embarrassment in front of peers, you can build a better relationship.

PRIVATE JOURNALS

Another strategy we've seen expert teachers utilize is a private journal that goes back and forth between the teacher and student. The student creates a notebook or journal in which they write or draw private thoughts, worries, and ideas. The student then turns in the book to the teacher at the end of the week so the teacher can write safe and reassuring messages to the student in response.

Several students have shared that this approach has helped them feel comfortable and safe, trusting adults in a less intimidating way than face-to-face conversation. Additionally, this can teach students a long-term life skill of journaling or creating art related to personal experiences. Writing, drawing, and journaling about experiences can reduce the impact of trauma.[89] One way to offer even further confidentiality and safety is to allow the student to fold the notebook page in half and staple it shut if the content is especially private and she doesn't want the teacher to read it.

---

89   van der Kolk, *The Body Keeps Score*, 243.

For younger students, teachers may staple blank pages together into a book that the child can bring home. Then, if things are stressful or traumatic in the home environment, they can access the notebook to create a drawing or write down thoughts. One of our teachers even put a picture of herself with the student on the front of the book as a reminder that she cares about him even when he's not at school. Think of this as another layer in building that foundation of safety and connection.

CREATE A CALMING STRATEGIES CHECKLIST

It is important to identify the things that help us calm down. For older students, you may want to create a calming strategies checklist. Younger students could be interviewed or observed to see how they tend to seek self-calm. Older students can begin to self-identify the things that help them become calm most effectively. When you take into account the student's individual interests and needs, you build a further relationship with the student. Consider items such as:

» Chewing gum

» Drawing or doodling

» Eating a snack

» Getting a drink of water

» Going for a walk

» Going to the "safe space" in the classroom

» Listening to music

» Reading a preferred book

» Sitting in an alternate location to work

» Smelling a preferred scent

» Standing up to work

» Squeezing a stress ball

» Taking a break

» Talking to a friend

» Talking to a preferred staff member

» Using a sensory or fidget toy

» Using a swing

» Using earplugs to block out noise

» Watching a sand timer

CALMING STRATEGIES

What types of calming strategies do you feel comfortable teaching your students to use? Can these options be put into a student checklist? How will they learn these strategies and access them when needed? Consider a quick classroom activity to teach available options and appropriate use.

CONSIDER REINFORCEMENT INVENTORIES

Another way to further develop relationships with students is to use reinforcement inventories to gather preferences on rewards and acknowledgements. Ask these questions in order to gather data on what a student might like to work for or earn based on behavioral or academic goals. Younger students can often pick from a forced choice question such as, "Would you rather earn a sticker or a snack?" whereas older students might be able to complete a ranked list of items provided or offer additional suggestions. Some common choices of what students like to learn often show up on reinforcement inventories:

» Access to technology

» Break time from work

» Dismissed early from class one day

» First choice of classroom job for the day

» First in line for lunch

» Free tardy pass

» Free time with a preferred adult at school

» Get an award certificate to bring home

» Get a thumbs up from a staff member

» Have good work posted publicly

» Help the teacher clean or prepare a task

» Homework pass

» Play a game with a friend

» Preferred music while working

» Preferred snack

» Send a positive message to the family

» Wear a hat for the day

Many reinforcement inventories have been created for students of all ages. For your youngest learners or those who are unable to read, you can read them the inventory, ask them to choose between two items, or place two items in front of them to see which one they select. This simple preference indication gives you an idea of something the child may be willing to earn or work toward when frustrated. Please refer to the Los Angeles Unified School District's Student Reinforcement Survey and Z. Z. Potential Reinforcer Survey. Both are available on the Los Angeles Unified School District website, https://achieve.lausd.net/domain/4.

GIVE UNDIVIDED ATTENTION

Throughout all of these relationship building practices, it is crucial to provide the student with true undivided attention. Modern students are often very aware of whether or not adults are actually paying attention, especially if they have experience in unsafe environments in which they feel the need to monitor adult behaviors and moods. We've started to notice that students begin to demonstrate more disruptive and connection-seeking behaviors as soon as adults look at an electronic device. When a caregiver pulls out a phone, the child often begins attempting to seek connection. Take a few seconds to think about whether you're offering undivided attention during your student interactions. Your relationship will provide a higher level of safety and connection if you are fully engaged with the individual.

Please keep in mind that relationship building should occur when both you and the child are calm. Be careful to not provide too much warm or positive attention when the student is off-task or engaged in disruptive behaviors. This response may inadvertently reinforce the problematic behavior by providing positive adult attention.

Another step to relationship building is to notice and repair your own mistakes. If you reflect on a situation with a student or staff member and feel like you could've handled it differently or more calmly, talk to the other person about this reflection. Admit your fault and work to repair the relationship before future situations arise. We have watched this approach work wonders between individuals in the school environment.

✓CHAPTER CHECKLIST
Building Genuine Relationships

Consider the strategies discussed in this chapter. Choose the strategies that you would like to begin implementing, then identify potential target students and a time of day or routine in which you can incorporate these new habits.

- ❑ Co-regulate to calm.
- ❑ Use two-by-tens.
- ❑ Give individual greetings.
- ❑ Learn the cultural differences of your students.
- ❑ Build positive family contacts.
- ❑ Strive for cooperation.
- ❑ Develop silent prompts/requests.
- ❑ Create private journals.
- ❑ Create a calming strategies checklist.
- ❑ Consider reinforcement inventories.
- ❑ Give undivided attention.

PART FOUR
POSITIVE PRACTICES AND UNIVERSAL SUPPORTS

CHAPTER 9

TEACH AND REINFORCE
EXPECTATIONS

As we begin to introduce positive practices and universal supports, try to conceptualize these as a group of strategies that can be used proactively in supporting your students and their behavior. These can be strategies that you plan to use right out of the gate and also, a source of problem-solving ideas that can be turned to when additional interventions or structures are needed for your class or for individual students. We are including a wide range of approaches and techniques that are rooted in best practices, and that we have seen to be successful for teachers and students. You will not always know who needs support, who might be suffering currently, or who might be triggered by past events, so we included supports that are likely to be helpful to all students. This does not mean that these practices are a good fit for all teachers and classrooms.

We have included far too many supports here to be implemented at once. Think about the needs of your students and the structures already in place at your school. Consider what is a good fit for your classroom community and your style as an educator. Modify terminology to fit the culture of your school and the culture of your students. Be aware that the following practices are positive techniques, both because they generally help students know what to do at any moment and because they are non-coercive and provide opportunities for positive reinforcement and relationship building. Lastly, have some fun with these practices; give yourself permission to be goofy as you keep building a positive culture in your classroom that helps students feel safe and connected.

Specific to teaching and reinforcing expectations, all too often educators make the mistake of assuming that students know what is expected, know when it is expected, and that they are motivated to perform what is expected. We often hear people lament student and family shortcomings around this topic when they would best spend their time and energy proactively addressing it in their school environment. Here are some approaches that work:

EXPLICITLY TELL, SHOW, PRACTICE, AND GIVE FEEDBACK

As we mentioned in Chapter 7, posting your positively stated expectations or rules is an important support. Beyond this, you must actively teach and practice those expectations. You can also teach, post, and practice routines and procedures. Routines and procedures are more specific to time and place and can include behavior chains such as how to line up, how to enter the classroom, how to request help, etc.

The recommended instructional methods for teaching expectations and routines and procedures are very similar. You can look to behavioral skills training (BST) for some guidance on how to teach, model, practice, and give feedback and reinforcement. Start with telling students what is expected and when. We recommend including a reason at this point. Veteran educators tell us that students now need more of a "why" when learning something new. After you "tell" a student what they are to do and provide a reason why they should do it, you can move to modeling or the "show" phase of training. Having students model the correct behavior can be powerful.

After you "tell" and "show" what needs to be done, move on to having students practice or "do" the behavior or routine. This is an important phase that is often overlooked. We cannot just tell our students how to perform a behavior and expect them to understand and generalize the correct behavior in other settings. Rather, students need to practice new behaviors where they will be expected to perform them. A common example would be teaching bus evacuations. We do not simply teach these in the classroom and expect students to know what to do once on the bus and in an emergency. Instead, we teach the evacuation routine and then practice on actual buses. That practice on the bus makes it more likely that students will perform the correct procedure at the right time.

How you have your students practice or "do" is important as well. We suggest procedures similar to errorless learning. With errorless learning, you do not allow the students to finish the practice with mistakes. If, during practice, the student starts to do the wrong thing, stop or prompt them to ensure the behavior is finished correctly. You may choose to let small errors go unprompted to be addressed later, but we advise you to stop and redirect any major errors the moment they occur. Practice until your students can demonstrate the behavior or procedure fluently without your corrections. Finally, after you "tell," "show," and have them "do," you need to give feedback. If you did not use errorless learning procedures or let minor errors slide, now is also the time to give corrective feedback. Please remember to give a high rate of positive reinforcement or acknowledgment. This will make it more likely that you see the correct behavior again in the future.

After your positively stated expectations are taught, modeled, practiced, reinforced, and posted in the classroom, you will still need to review them from time to time. A proactive practice is to review your expectations after breaks in instruction like after spring break or long weekends. When new students join your classroom, it is an excellent opportunity to reteach and review expectations, routines, and procedures. Your existing students can also serve as the models for new students. This quickly establishes the culture of your classroom for new students as they see current students doing the "right thing." Oftentimes, we hear that students who may not always make the right choices can prove to be very effective models.

Another important time to review, reteach, and practice is when the behavior of your class starts to erode. You can choose to review some or all of your expectations, routines, and procedures. You should find that this process will go faster than your original instruction. Think of your original instruction and any reteaching as a time investment. You will get that time back in dealing with fewer problem behaviors and having more efficient transitions.

USE A RATIO OF 5:1 POSITIVE INTERACTIONS TO NEGATIVE CORRECTIONS

Having a high ratio of positive contacts to negative contacts is closely related to the rationale for using positively stated expectations. Here we are really talking about rates of reinforcement versus punishment. The research for this has wider implications than just what happens in the classroom, extending to how it relates to high and low performing business teams.[90] There are also implications for adult relationships. Researchers have correlated rates of positive and negative verbal interactions and affect for newlywed couples and found a high accuracy in predicting who would divorce and stay together.[91] What we know about classrooms is that if you have a high ratio (5:1) of positive adult to student interactions versus a classroom environment that has higher rates of reprimands, you see fewer behavioral disruptions and more academic engagement.[92] Similarly, when you need to give constructive feedback to a student, a history of positive acknowledgments will make any reprimand more meaningful.

There is one important caveat: this is not a 5:1 ratio per student. There are some students whose current behavioral patterns would preclude using this ratio. Instead, the goal is to reach this ratio for your class as a whole. Keeping the ratio high for the class as a whole does have an impact on individual students. Every time you publicly acknowledge a student for engaging in appropriate behavior, you are reminding other students of what is expected of them. You are signaling that students get teacher attention for doing the right thing.

---

90   Jack Zenger and Joseph Folkman, "The Ideal Praise-to-Criticism Ratio," *Harvard Business Review*, March 15, 2013, https://hbr.org/2013/03/the-ideal-praise-to-criticism.

91   John M. Gottman et al., "Predicting Marital Happiness and Stability from Newlywed Interactions," *Journal of Marriage and Family* 60, no. 1 (February 1998): 5–22.

92   Clayton R. Cook et al., "Evaluating the Impact of Increasing General Education Teachers' Ratio of Positive-to-Negative Interactions on Students' Classroom Behavior," *Journal of Positive Behavior Interventions* 19, no. 2 (2017): 67–77.

One strategy to keep your ratio of positive to negative contacts high is to consider the technique of proximity or vicarious reinforcement. This is one of our favorite techniques for classroom management and one with which we have seen great success. Proximity reinforcement can be used when minor and undangerous problem behaviors are noticed. Instead of correcting the offending student directly, we give reinforcement to a student near the one exhibiting the behavior problem. For example, if Susie is talking instead of getting started on a task, but her table mate Javier is on task, you might give behavior-specific praise to Javier by approaching the table and stating, "Javier, thank you for being on task by getting started quickly." This is even more powerful if getting started quickly was previously taught as a positive behavioral expectation. If you have a class- or school-wide reinforcement system, this would be a time to pair a reinforcer with your praise for Javier. For example, if Susie picked up on the cue to start working, you can reinforce her behavior right in the moment as well.

Another benefit of keeping your rate of positive acknowledgements high and using proximity reinforcement is that you can catch students who are usually doing the right thing. Sometimes educators forget to acknowledge these students, but if you reinforce their good behavior at times, then they are more likely to keep doing the correct behavior. This is akin to intermittent reinforcement (Chapter 6). When we *sometimes* are reinforced for our behavior, that behavior is likely to be continued or endure. Think back to our example about gamblers in Las Vegas. The gambling industry is full of behavioral experts, and their goal is to keep you betting. Slot machines are fine-tuned to keep those that engage in that behavior sitting in that seat and plunking in coins. It works because *sometimes* that behavior pays off with a win, even though in the long run you are destined to lose.

 INCREASING REINFORCEMENTS

Reflect on your overall interactions with students. Do you think you are generally initiating five positive interactions for every negative or corrective interaction? How could you build more reinforcement or acknowledgement into your day to get closer to that ratio?

PRAISE PUBLICLY (USUALLY)

Publicly acknowledging students who meet behavioral expectations holds power for the individual student as well as the whole class. By doing this, we signal to students how to get the powerful reinforcer of adult attention. You also give children an avenue to get that attention, when for some, they could seek peer attention for negative behaviors as an alternative. However, we do want to caution that some students do not like public praise from the teacher. This is important to discuss in light of practices that support students with a traumatic background. Some students may come to you with little experience getting attention for displaying positive behaviors. Some children get most of their adult attention by demonstrating problem behaviors. We have seen this pattern with children coming from homes where we suspected abuse, traumatic experiences, or when there were many children with few adult resources.

Sadly, for some students, their primary method to gain adult attention is through creating problems. Some students will bring this behavioral pattern into the classroom. These escalating behaviors can be quite shocking and provocative, where students have learned to up the ante over time to get attention or to escape unwanted consequences. You may also encounter students who have established a behavioral pattern of accessing peer attention through being the "bad" kid. This pattern is often seen when students have other shortcomings such as poor academic skills. Being the "bad" kid gets you better quality peer attention than being the "dumb" student. If you praise this type of student publicly, you may inadvertently be messing with their self-image and method for commanding respect from their peers.

If you have a student who is uncomfortable with public praise, you may learn this through their reactions in the moment. They may talk back, almost as though trying to initiate a power struggle, or they may show discomfort by showing you a problem behavior quickly after being praised. For example, the student praised for working quietly might call out immediately after. If you encounter students like this, try to make an extra effort to build a closer relationship with them. Consider a technique like the Two-by-Ten procedure that was discussed in Chapter 8. You can also praise this student privately or more covertly. This will largely be about building trust, and your student will need to feel safe with you in the role of reinforcer. You may consider, as your relationship builds, establishing a nonverbal signal to use when you want to let the student know that they are doing the right thing.

ISSUE QUICK REINFORCEMENT

We know that reinforcement makes behavior more likely to happen in the future under similar circumstances. We also know that being behavior-specific (labeling exactly what the student did right) makes reinforcement more effective. Now we want to talk about optimizing positive reinforcement by highlighting the timing of the delivery. Immediacy is a term that is often used to describe this dimension of reinforcement. It can be at its most powerful when delivered within seconds, or even during, the behavior you want to increase. This is not to say that reinforcement delivered later is bad; it is not, it is just less effective.

To reinforce behaviors quickly, you can use positive verbal behavior-specific praise. We see teachers use this very effectively while students are doing the right thing. For example, "I see Letisha is working hard and I like how Devon is using his dictionary to look up spelling words." This works well if students find verbal praise valuable. You can also use tokens or placeholders that can be offered in the moment and then exchanged for backup reinforcers at a later time. We encourage you to issue reinforcement quickly, especially when students are learning new behaviors or when they begin to display more appropriate behaviors. In these cases, use a high rate of positive reinforcement, maybe acknowledging every instance at first, letting students know they are doing the right thing as soon as possible following the initiation or completion of the desired behavior. In general, positive reinforcement is a powerful tool to help teach and maintain appropriate behavior.

CONSIDER GROUP CONTINGENCIES

Group contingencies can be a powerful source of motivation and reinforcement, and they are seemingly underutilized in schools. All group contingencies involve setting a criterion to earn reinforcement, whether students earn that as each one meets the criteria, when all of them meet that criteria, or when only one student or subgroup meets the criteria. Group contingencies can help a group of students cooperate on specific tasks or toward the same goal. While there are several types of group contingencies, we will just give a few examples of successful implementations from schools. Occasionally, you may find that you have a student who finds value in the negative attention that comes from ruining the contingency for the rest of the group. If you have one of those students, set up contingencies so that the reinforcement does not rely on that one student's performance.

An astonishing example of a group contingency that we observed took place in a junior high special education classroom. This class had a number of students with significant traumatic backgrounds and was not typically a population we believed worked well together. The teacher taught the students the expectations and routine of how to switch the classroom desks from rows to small groups and how to get materials prepared and put away for small group lessons. The reinforcer for this contingency was to earn preferred activity time (PAT) on Fridays. Upon her signal, the teacher would start a timer with a goal length or several minutes for rearranging the room; any time left over would be banked for Friday PAT. After each of these transitions, the teacher would add the time saved to a total on the whiteboard. The results were miraculous and the group of students worked together wonderfully.

Another example of an effective group contingency is to tally toward a set amount of acknowledgment tickets, tokens, or points that students receive outside of the classroom. Students can pick a reinforcer like an activity or special snack to work toward and then everyone can earn the reinforcer based on good behavior. Group contingencies can also be set for all students but earned individually. For example, when each student finishes an assignment satisfactorily, that student can engage in a preferred activity such as reading.

TEACH SOCIAL PROBLEM-SOLVING TECHNIQUES

All students can have peer-to-peer difficulties at times. You can try to get ahead of some of these difficulties by teaching social problem-solving strategies. For example, you can teach standard responses to difficulties in peer interactions like teasing or minor disagreements. Some evidence-based bully prevention curricula also include teaching potential victims and bystanders some tools to use.[93] Part of that curricula introduces three responses (stop, walk, and talk) to all students. It teaches students that if they receive any unwanted interactions from others, they can respond with a "stop" word or phrase and a signal such as holding up their hand. If implemented, you would teach all students to recognize this as a sign to stop an interaction. Some students may not know that they are giving unwanted attention to their peers, so using this technique may solve some issues before they progress. Students are then taught to walk away if the unwanted interaction continues past the stop signal. If that does not work, then the next step is to go report to an adult. While this would be more ideal as a school-wide approach, giving some similar strategies to your class could be helpful.

Another technique that has shown a good deal of promise in teaching students to solve minor disagreements is the rock, paper, scissors approach. Teachers are reporting that this is successful on the playground to solve disagreements like deciding if a ball was over the line or who gets a preferred item of equipment next. We are seeing this then spill into other school environments, helping with other potential areas of conflict like being first in line or who gets the water fountain next. Students may even start to use this strategy on their own. If you highlight that students have a small problem and then prompt them to solve it with rock, paper, scissors, this may also help them recognize small versus big issues.

TEACH STUDENTS A BREATHING STRATEGY

Many social-emotional programs teach specific breathing strategies to use with students. The basic idea is that deep inhales stimulate action and deep exhales promote calm. In order to activate the brain and body, you can prompt students to take several long, deep inhales. This stimulates energy flow throughout the individual. On the flip side, to create a more calm and relaxed energy, focus on slow, long exhales. For example, you could prompt everyone to breathe in to the count of three and exhale to the count of six. This could be done as a group activity after a more active routine but before the need to sit still and focus on another activity.

---

93 · "Materials," Positive Behavioral Interventions and Supports, accessed January 7, 2020, https://www.pbis.org/resource-type/materials#bullying-prevention.

The best way to incorporate these strategies into your classroom is to practice while everyone is calm.

Even if you have not previously taught students a breathing strategy while everyone is calm, you can still model it during a stressful moment. The human brain has mirror neurons—brain cells that subconsciously notice how others are behaving and trigger the body to model after that behavior. This is the same mechanism that causes you to yawn after the person next to you yawns. This is also related to the concept of co-regulation we previously discussed. You can use this natural reaction to your advantage when you are dealing with a student who demonstrates agitated behaviors. Educators can model calm behavior by keeping their voice levels low and slow, breathing deeply, and moving around the room peacefully. We have used this technique countless times with agitated students and they tend to de-escalate much faster than when we appear anxious and stressed ourselves. Eventually, those mirror neurons start working and the child begins to deepen her breath to match the adult's breath.

As we've discussed previously, humans revert to brain stem or limbic functioning when they are triggered or feel unsafe. Those parts of the brain where calming strategies are stored will shut down when you feel threatened. The more threatened you feel, the less likely you are to access those calming strategies. In these moments, we need to rely on someone or something in our environment to cue us back to these strategies. For example, sending a student to the safe space in the room without a staff member or safe buddy might not be effective. That student who is triggered at the moment may require an additional person to join them and breathe with them or help them choose a calming strategy. Think back to our discussions on your own self-regulation and body awareness to make sure you are modeling calm breathing and body awareness with your students.

✓CHAPTER CHECKLIST
Teach and Reinforce Expectations

❏ Explicitly teach, model, practice, and reinforce expectations.

❏ Use a ratio of 5:1 positive interactions to negative corrections.

❏ Praise publicly (usually).

❏ Issue quick reinforcement.

❏ Consider group contingencies.

❏ Teach social problem-solving techniques.

❏ Teach students a breathing strategy.

CHAPTER 10

PROMPTING STRATEGIES

Once we have taught our students what is expected, we need to think about how we can get them to display those desired behaviors at the right times. Some students will be quick to show you, while others may need a little or a lot of prompting. Below are a few concepts and strategies to help make your prompting and your students successful.

PROMPT STUDENTS WITH WHAT TO DO (AVOID NO, DON'T, AND STOP)

Arguably, the single most important thing we can do to help support students who are struggling with their behavior is to use language or picture prompts that tell them explicitly what to do. This can be a difficult shift as it is not how most people normally speak. When adults change how they give directives and corrections to students, there is often a large change in student behavior. We speak from experience, having worked to change behavioral and management systems at the individual, classroom, program, and school level. One example from Jon's experience involves program change for two classrooms that support students with significant emotional and behavioral difficulties. Before changing the language of the adults (along with teaching and reinforcing expectations), staff were physically restraining students on a nearly daily basis. Once adults changed their language in explicitly teaching behaviors and interacting with students, the program was restraint-free for a year and a half. Similarly, at the school level, we have found adults reporting lower levels of problem behavior once reminders and redirections moved from "no, don't, and stop" to directives like "safe hands" and "use kind words."

We encourage you to do three things: 1) give students instructions and directions that explicitly tell them what to do, 2) use positively stated language to redirect minor misbehavior, and 3) when correcting or redirecting students, as much as possible, take "no," "don't," and "stop" out of your vocabulary. We want to emphasize the importance of teaching student behavioral expectations using positively stated language and also the problems that come with rules that only tell what not to do. It behooves you to assume that your students do not know what is expected because some of them do not know or, if they do know, they have not generalized those expectations to the school setting.

Using positively stated language for redirection or error correction has some additional rationale. Simply put, you get more of what you give attention to. For example, if you reprimand talking out and label that problem behavior in your error correction, the student's talking out may stop, but usually only temporarily. The command to stop talking is also a cue to other students to talk out. You may have inadvertently signaled that talking out is a way to get teacher attention. This is difficult for educators at times because it is counterintuitive and reprimands do get reinforced in the moment with a temporary cessation of the student's problem behavior.

Earlier we suggested an exercise of reframing unwanted behaviors into their positive opposites. The same logic applies here. For students who are talking out, you can redirect them with a reminder that the expectation is to work quietly. Even better, as we will discuss in more detail later, consider praising students who are working quietly before giving your attention to students who are not meeting that expectation. Other examples might include prompting the expectation of "listen respectfully" instead of reprimanding with "stop talking." You can prompt the use of "respectful words" instead of giving too much attention to "inappropriate language."

Using positively stated language works for a number of reasons. One reason is that humans often think in pictures. For example, when we are told not to think of a pink elephant, most of us immediately picture a pink elephant in our minds. We want corrections to create a mental picture of the expected behavior (e.g., walking instead of running). Our colleagues in the field of speech-language pathology have also taught us that young children do not hear negations until a certain stage in their development. For our young learners, "no running" might really just be a prompt to run. Instead, just consider a verbal prompt of "walking feet" or showing a picture cue of walking; even better pair the picture cue with the positively stated verbal prompt.

Using prompts is a good way to ensure a new skill or a good decision gets reinforced. It is also a great technique to get some traction with students who are struggling with behavior. We like to think of it as a learning trial. When you prompt a student right in the moment or right before a behavior is expected, and then immediately acknowledge that correct behavior, you will be more likely to see that behavior again, hopefully with less prominent prompting. For example, you can prompt hand raising nonverbally right before or as a student is calling out and then enthusiastically praise them for hand raising. You can remind a student to ask for help just before you give them a difficult task and then praise asking for help while making sure you get them that help quickly. In this manner, you can set your students up for success with well-timed prompts.

PRE-TEACH AND PRE-CORRECT

Pre-teaching and pre-correcting are key practices for preventing behavior difficulties in the classroom and other school environments. Too often we assume that children know what is expected of them and then when they fail to live up to those expectations, we have traditionally punished them. When you are proactive in making expectations clear, you are more likely to get the behavior you want and you will have increased opportunities to reinforce those expected behaviors, thus making them more likely to happen next time.

Think of pre-teaching as an investment in which you regain that time in smoother operation of the classroom. You can pair that explicit instruction with prompts and pre-corrections to remind students of the steps in a routine when you know that behavioral mistakes might be likely. Teachers are frequently prompting and pre-correcting behaviors for their students in the most well-managed classrooms. For example, when lining up, you can outline the steps and expectations just before you anticipate students to display those behaviors.

In our personal experience, these techniques are invaluable when supervising students with trauma exposure or behavioral difficulties. For example, when we know that the lunch line can be a hotspot for behavioral difficulties, we might stop our students and remind them of the expectations for getting their lunch and getting to the correct table. When supervising dismissal, we get the attention of the class and then review the procedure for lining up and leaving to the buses. In each of these examples, acknowledging students for making the correct choices in the moment, even though they were just reminded, is a powerful tool to increase the likelihood of getting the correct behavior again in the future.

PRE-CORRECTING ROUTINES

Think about any particular routines or transitions that tend to be problematic for your students. How can you incorporate pre-teaching and/or pre-correction ahead of these times?

USE SHORT, CLEAR DIRECTIONS PAIRED WITH VISUAL PROMPTS

There are a number of reasons to keep directions and redirections short and clear. Students who have receptive language issues, developmental delays, autism spectrum disorder needs, or who are English language learners may always need verbal content to be simplified or supplemented with visual cues. You will also encounter students who get frustrated and whose behavior may escalate when teachers direct lots of language at them. We recommend that you generally use an economy of words (e.g., "sit" or "nice hands") when giving directions or corrections. Also, consider using gestures or visual prompts when possible, especially if you suspect that excess language is escalating a student's behavior. Be careful with multistep directions. Some students have memory deficits and too many directions at once can be frustrating and counterproductive to them. Also remember that when a student is triggered into an emotional or survival state, they have less ability to process words or language.

NONVERBAL PROMPTING

At times, nonverbal or visual prompts are the preferred approach. Some of these instances occur when you are supporting students who are deaf, hearing impaired, nonverbal, or learning a new language. For other students, you may want to supplement with nonverbal prompts if verbally responding to their problem behaviors is reinforcing or escalating that behavior. We caution against pointing at students, as some students interpret this as disrespectful and, thus, it could make the situation worse.

As we discussed in "Create a Safe and Supportive Environment," it is good practice to post prompts for routines and procedures. These are visual prompts that you can direct student attention toward rather than having to engage in verbal discussion. The hope would be for students to independently access help by referring back to those prompts. Other common nonverbal prompts include pointing to a student's seat if they wander, pointing to or tapping on a students' assignment if their attention wanes, or modeling hand raising if a student calls out.

For students whose behavior may escalate with repeated verbal directions, we have had success with writing a brief prompt on a personal white board or making a list on paper. If you use lists, you can direct students to choose what item to start with and then have them cross off each completed item. There are also systems for using picture cues to communicate and build language. These are typically employed for teaching students with developmental disabilities, but the pictures can be good for prompting a wide range of students. A common example might be to point to the "quiet" picture to cue or redirect a student to work quietly rather than verbally telling them to do so.

NONVERBAL PROMPTS

What types of nonverbal prompts can you build into your student interactions?

VISUAL CHOICE BOARDS

A visual choice board is a form of prompting that also includes issuing choice (covered in more detail in Chapter 13). It is a great technique for gaining compliance when working with students with verbal or language deficits and for students who do not respond well to additional verbal engagement. We have seen these used very effectively in a planned and routine manner and also in the moment as a fallback method to prompt students to make a choice.

A visual choice board is a board that utilizes picture prompts or brief written prompts, depending on your student. They can be simple laminated sheets or a board with removable Velcro pictures. Some teachers use individual white boards with written choices and then ask their students to point to their desired choice. Teachers can maintain instructional control in this manner by setting acceptable options as choices, while students can gain autonomy by having the ability to choose throughout the day.

EYE GAZES

Related to nonverbal prompting, many teachers use a "look" or eye gaze to redirect student behavior. This technique is more powerful when a strong and trusting relationship has been built. In that case, eye gaze may be able to offer a sense of comfort or support as well. We will caution here that a long gaze or staring may be perceived as disrespectful or aggressive. It is important to know your students. Students with social deficits, like those on the autism spectrum, may not respond well or at all to the use of eye gaze.

TRANSITION AND ATTENTION SIGNALS

Transition signals, attention signals, and quiet signals are very helpful for classroom management. The signals here are varied. You can get creative and match them to your classroom culture. What is vital is that they are well taught and practiced and that once in place, you are consistent in your expectations that all students routinely follow the signal. If some students are having trouble following the signal, do not struggle on this point. Instead, maintain your instructional flow and transition the majority of your class before addressing the students who are struggling.

The signals can take many forms. Some teachers use an easily accessible chime, bell, or other noise. Many teachers use a word or phrase (e.g., 1-2-3 eyes on me). Others use a call and response (e.g., teacher: "class class," students: "yes yes"). Sometimes you may need to repeat the signal to get everyone's attention, but make sure to issue positive reinforcement whenever your class responds correctly. Once you have the attention of the entire class, you can give directions with a higher likelihood of your students understanding and following along.

FIRST-THEN BOARDS

There are a number of terms for the first-then approach, such as when-then, if-then, etc. What they all have in common is that when you use them, you are setting up a contingency. When one thing happens, then this other thing is next. We typically present a First-Then contingency to build motivation to complete a task. It is especially useful when task initiation is difficult. We offer reinforcement with a desired task in order to make completing a less-desired activity more appealing. We often see teachers use a visual if-then display board. This can look different depending on the skill and developmental level of your students. Sometimes you may use a picture cue for both the "If" and "Then." For more advanced students, you might write down the activities or items. For some students you can let them choose the "Then" activity or item. You can let students choose from a menu or you can simply offer two choices (e.g., five minutes of iPad or go for a walk). Once you start getting more work from students, you can expand on the "If" part of the contingency. For example, you might move to a "1-2-3, Done" format in which you expect three pieces of work to be completed before reinforcement.

You might use this approach in your own life. If you don't already, you may want to give it a try. When we are faced with tasks we do not want to do, like cleaning the house or finishing our taxes, we sometimes identify things to reward ourselves. For instance, we might set a contingency that after cleaning the kitchen we will stream an episode of our favorite comedy or eat a bowl of ice cream. This is often referred to as the Premack Principle. Consider giving it a try next time you are dreading tackling that stack of papers or getting yourself to the gym.

✓CHAPTER CHECKLIST
Prompting Strategies

Here is a list of considerations when using prompting strategies. The checklist serves as a quick reference of general practices to refer to as needed.

❑ Prompt students with what TO DO (avoid no, don't, and stop).

❑ Pre-teach and pre-correct.

❑ Use short, clear directions paired with visual prompts.

❑ Use nonverbal prompting.

❑ Use visual choice boards.

❑ Use eye gaze.

❑ Use transition and attention signals.

❑ Use first-then boards.

CHAPTER 11

BODY POSITIONING AND **VOICE**

How you move, position your body, and use your voice are powerful tools to support student behavior. While many other approaches require materials or planning, the tools we discuss in this chapter are always at your disposal and easily extend outside of the classroom.

ACTIVE SUPERVISION

Active supervision is an important best practice for preventing behavioral difficulties and maintaining a safe environment in the classroom or in other school settings such as the playground. This practice involves continuously scanning, moving, and interacting with students. We talked about room setup and the importance of being able to see every part of your instructional space from every other part of the classroom. Making frequent visual scans of the classroom or other educational environment allows you to prevent problem behaviors from occurring since students know that supervision is always likely. You will be able to see where problems are about to develop, either with an individual student or with a potentially problematic interaction between students. At this point you may be able to simply use your eye gaze or "teacher look" (typically eyebrows raised and an expression that conveys "you better not") to stop problems in their tracks. Alternatively, this may be the time to approach students to offer support or issue private redirections.

Moving around the environment is another important part of active supervision. It is advised to frequently move and to do so in an unpredictable pattern. Along with visual scans, moving in an unpredictable pattern can suppress or prevent problem behaviors as students will know that they may be under supervision at any time. We have seen that lack of movement, either with the adults sitting in one place in the classroom or standing in one location in the cafeteria or at recess, creates spaces where students are more likely to engage in problem behaviors. Students can often tell you about such spaces on a school campus, such as in the corner of the recess field or the back corner of a particular classroom. Moving often and in irregular patterns can prevent these problems from arising to some degree.

The third tenet of active supervision is interacting with students. These interactions can take many forms—from relationship building to error correction. Relationship building with students should be a continuous process, and this can be furthered during supervision by making conversation, noticing things like new shoes, a haircut, or a sports jersey, and checking in on their lives. This is a great time to find out about student interests. Interacting during active supervision is also a time to offer support. If you see a student who appears to be having difficulty with peers, a task, or with managing emotions, you can offer support using an empathetic approach. You may see signs in your students that look like withdrawal, frustration, or even behavioral excesses like pacing or talking loudly. This is a great time to offer help, prompt students to problem solve, offer choice, or provide a calming activity to prevent behavioral escalation. When interacting with students during active supervision, you can also redirect any problem behaviors that have started by reminding students of what's expected of them. Acknowledging good behavior during your interactions through reinforcement, with behavior-specific praise or another more formal reinforcement system (tickets, points, etc.), is like preventative medicine that can keep problem behaviors at bay.

Are there any particular routines, independent work periods, or small group activity times during which you could increase your active supervision to support student behavior?

GET ON YOUR STUDENT'S LEVEL/HEIGHT AND APPROACH FROM THE FRONT-SIDE ANGLE

When you have any individual interactions with students other than quick acknowledgments or brief directions or redirections, it is generally a good idea to get on their level. Try to bend at the knees, giving adequate personal space, while positioning yourself to ensure you can move away quickly if needed. It is much less threatening to smaller and younger students when you get down to their level. Getting down to a student's level also allows you to give corrective feedback in a more private manner that conveys respect. In general, and especially in thinking about students who may have experienced trauma at the hands of adults, by lowering yourself you can hope to avoid potentially triggering students by inadvertently intimidating them with your size and potentially sparking fight-or-flight responses.

Approaching from the front-side angle is also an important consideration, especially for students with trauma exposure. Try not to approach or enter a student's space from behind. Imagine someone much larger than you surprising you by being in your space by coming from behind. This could easily be unsettling for anyone. Likewise, be careful about approaching directly from the front. Being squared off with someone in front of you can easily be interpreted as aggressive. If possible, approach from the front-side angle and in view of the individual.

ASK TO ENTER STUDENTS' SPACE OR TOUCH MATERIALS

Another way to convey respect and avoid triggering students with potential trauma exposure is to ask before getting into their personal space or touching their things. Oftentimes we will be very vigilant in this approach when we get new students and do not yet know their history or behavioral tendencies. Asking to enter students' personal spaces or touch their materials often takes the form of offering help or assistance. For example, if you see students showing signs of frustration, you might ask if you can see what they are working on or ask if you can take a look. Getting the student's permission is very different from just taking something from their desk. Taking an item from students could trigger them into an emotional or survival state, and it is best if we take a more collaborative approach. You can use the same approach to help students with other tasks such as tying their shoes or opening their food containers. For some students, especially if there is a pattern of using problem behaviors to get needs met, you will want to prompt them to ask for help so that this becomes an established behavior for accessing your support.

MODEL APPROPRIATE VOLUME AND TONE FOR THE SETTING AND CIRCUMSTANCES

Modeling appropriate voice volume and tone is a technique to consider as you teach students appropriate behavior for a setting. It is also a technique to use when an individual's behavior starts to escalate. In general, you are always modeling for your students. It is a wonderful opportunity to make sure they are exposed to adults who are respectful, calm, and kind. This modeling can also help students learn to adapt to various educational environments. Many teachers are successful at demonstrating different inflections in certain settings, such as in the hallway, media center, and at recess; many are also successful when switching from various activities in the classroom. Your modeling of voice qualities only serves to strengthen that learning for students.

Modeling appropriate volume and tone is also important when a student's behavior escalates. All of us have a tendency to match each other in voice qualities such as volume, tone, and cadence. Over and over again we have witnessed interpersonal interactions where if one person gets loud in matching another, then the first person will increase their volume and so forth. This is one way that situations can escalate and power struggles intensify. On the other hand, we have seen many educators consciously keep their voice at an appropriate level for the setting they are in, sometimes purposely lowering it while projecting calm with their other voice qualities. When this happens, you can help to prevent further escalation and de-escalate students with your modeling. This also works when interacting with other adults, both in person or over the phone. It is difficult and awkward to escalate when the other person is not going along for the ride. Use the power of co-regulation to your benefit.

✓CHAPTER CHECKLIST
Body Positioning and Voice

Here is a list of considerations when using body positioning and voice. The checklist serves as a quick reference of general practices to refer to as needed.

❑ Use active supervision.

❑ Get on your student's level/height and approach from the front-side angle.

❑ Ask to enter a student's space or touch their materials.

❑ Model appropriate volume and tone for the setting and circumstances.

CHAPTER 12

PROVIDE
PREDICTABILITY

We both started our careers in positions that supported students with significant emotional and behavioral needs. Many of them had trauma exposure along with other challenges. At separate times and in different settings, we quickly learned the power of predictable and consistent environments in supporting those students.

PROVIDE PREDICTABLE ROUTINES

Consistency and predictability are helpful to all students (and adults as well). Predictability helps overcome anxiety; we do better when we know what is expected and what is coming next. We covered the need to post the steps of routines and the classroom schedule in the chapter on creating a safe and supportive environment. In this chapter we emphasize the need for consistency in your daily routines, as some students will likely struggle if those routines are in place on some days but not on others. Reasons for incorporating this practice include that students may become anxious or frustrated when things change (shrinking window of tolerance) while others may be reinforced by engaging in behaviors other than those prescribed by your routines. That intermittent reinforcement, where some behaviors or activities are acceptable on some days and not on others, can be powerful and lead to enduring misbehaviors. We need to watch ourselves to avoid drifting from our expectations and procedures. You also need to be prepared for changes beyond your control, such as half days, fire drills, or an internet outage. If those types of changes are coming, it is best to prepare your students for them as soon as possible.

As much as you want to maintain consistency and ensure predictability, there is a lot you cannot control. When you know changes to the schedule are coming, inform your students and prepare them as soon as possible. For individual students who struggle with unpredictability or noise, you may need to get creative to mitigate the effects of events like fire drills. In these cases, work with your administration. For example, we collaborated with a principal to help a student on the autism spectrum. The student assisted with setting off the first fire drill of the year, and was then warned ahead of time for the other occurrences.

CONSIDER INDIVIDUAL SCHEDULES

While individual schedules are often used with students on the autism spectrum, a wider range of students can benefit from the increased predictability of this approach. We know that having a predictable and consistent environment is helpful to all of us, but it can be particularly helpful for students with emotional or behavioral difficulties and exposure to trauma. It is easier to begin to build trust with those in the school environment if you know what is expected and what is going to happen next each day. This helps support safety and connection for students. Beyond having a classroom schedule, an individual schedule can be considered for students in need.

Individual schedules can take a number of forms. We often see laminated pictures of the day's activities that are stuck onto the schedule with Velcro. With this system, items are typically moved to a "finished" or "all done" column once completed. Another option is to simply write the schedule on paper and cross off items upon completion. As students get older and are able to self-manage, you can have them write their own schedule on paper. A very important part of any individual schedule system is to make sure to review it daily at the beginning of the day. Also, it must be used consistently and not only on some school days. Individual schedules can also give you a format for reinforcement. After each activity on a schedule, you can issue reinforcement or corrective feedback.

INDIVIDUAL SCHEDULES

Do any of your students need the support of an individual schedule? If so, what would it look like in your classroom (pictures, written schedule, to-do list)?

USE TIMERS TO BUILD PREDICTABILITY

We have had numerous teachers share that timers can function like magic in the classroom and, from our experience, we agree. Timers can help build predictability and give a sense of consistency. Larger visual timers help students predict when activities or breaks will end and smaller timers with an auditory ringing function work as well. With the advent of smartphones and watches, most of us typically have this tool on us or within the classroom. It is often a good practice to give students transition warnings (e.g., two more minutes of reading, then lunch) and setting a timer along with these warnings can be helpful. We have seen teachers give the timer to individual students who struggle with transitions along with the "job" of being the time keeper. In some instances, it is helpful to set a timer for the length of the desired activities. This has the benefit of building predictability, while also depersonalizing the termination of the activity. The timer can signal the end of the activity and that "rule" can help prevent power struggles. We sometimes teach individual students who struggle to transition from preferred activities to request more time as this is more acceptable than a tantrum or engaging in physical aggression. We can then give them one more minute or issue a choice like selecting one or two more minutes. In these instances, we like to set the timer and show it to the student as we start it.

✓CHAPTER CHECKLIST
Provide Predictability

Here is a list of considerations when providing predictability. The checklist serves as a quick reference of general practices to refer to as needed.

❑ Provide predictable routines and warn ahead of schedule changes, fire drills, assemblies.

❑ Consider individual schedules.

❑ Use timers to build predictability.

CHAPTER 13

SUPPORT INDIVIDUAL **NEEDS**

The past few chapters covered many universal classroom practices that work to support most student populations. In this chapter, we share additional strategies and accommodations to use proactively for individual students, small groups, or potentially, for your whole classroom if you serve a special population.

PROVIDE ADDITIONAL WAIT TIME

There are a number of reasons to give adequate wait time to students when you ask them to respond. These include being respectful of individual differences in processing skills for students who may have disabilities, allowing additional processing time for students who are learning a new language, and supporting students who may be exposed to trauma. Providing wait time is a skill that many adults struggle with and one that we have had to work on developing over time. It often feels very artificial to give extra processing time, but it can make all the difference. Try counting on your fingers for five to ten seconds in silence. It may feel like a long time and can seem awkward during interactions with another. In addition, some educators begin to feel anxious while they're waiting. Many adults come from a work ethic or family culture that makes them feel as though they should always be doing "something," whether that is solving the problem in front of them at the moment or getting back to the pacing of their academic instruction. Rest assured that you are doing something when you give wait time to students. During this time, you are allowing them to solve problems and make choices more independently. When students do make the right choice, you can reinforce their behavior, which will most likely encourage them to make good choices in the future with less need for wait time.

PROVIDE CHOICES

Providing choices to students is one of the best reactive behavioral techniques you can use in schools. You can also incorporate choice proactively so that students begin learning independence and autonomy, especially as they start reaching adolescence. You can maintain instructional control by directing them to tasks to be completed, while also building choice into those activities. For example, you may provide topics or themes, within parameters, for a particular writing assignment. You might offer them a choice in materials or colors to use. Some students may need choice embedded into activities to encourage good behavior.

Other types of choices may be more reactive in nature. For example, when students are having difficulty initiating a series of tasks, you might give them other types of choices, such as where to sit or what order in which to complete the series. Get creative here. Often the perception of having some choice can make the task feel less aversive. Other types of choices may come into play when you want to highlight potential consequences. For example, you can frame behavioral decisions as a choice, but we suggest being very careful in how you present those options. If a student perceives that this is a coercive threat (e.g., do this or else), you may be inviting a power struggle or an escalated emotional or behavioral reaction. You also need to be careful in highlighting any potential punishment consequences; they need to be of appropriate magnitude and you must be able to follow through with them. Some examples of appropriate choices might sound like: "I really want you to earn your points this hour, you can earn them if you choose to follow directions. I will give you a minute to decide." Another example might be, "You can choose to attempt your math now or we can work on it during free time, you choose." As always, if students make the right choice, remember to acknowledge that with approval or another type of reinforcement.

Think about the choices you are willing to allow during classroom routines and for particular students. Where can you build more choices into your day?

PROVIDE SENSORY TOOLS: VESTIBULAR, PROPRIOCEPTIVE, AND TOUCH SYSTEMS

Many of our students experience difficulty with sensory regulation in the educational environment. This is a common response of the body after a traumatic experience occurs. Even students who aren't exposed to traumatic experiences may demonstrate these needs. Any of the following sensory strategies may help the student expand their window of tolerance when triggered by a certain event or when faced with difficult routines. You may want to consult with an occupational therapist if your students require this type of support frequently. An occupational therapist would provide further resources in this area than we are providing.

Sensory approaches are often framed in the context of vestibular, proprioceptive, and touch systems. Each of these systems impacts how an individual interprets sensory information from their environment. When one or more systems are dysregulated, the individual will likely experience a decreased window of tolerance.

The vestibular system operates from inner ear mechanisms and impacts a person's perception of their body position and movement. This system is sometimes referred to as a person's inner GPS system,[94] anchoring them to spatial awareness.

---

94 Champagne, "Sensory Modulation."

Proprioception is the system that senses a person's movement against resistance. This system anchors the body to space, time, and body awareness. Strategies that target this system help the brain override the hyperarousal and anxiety responses. These strategies may include:

- Bouncing on a medicine ball
- Jumping on a trampoline
- Playing sports
- Pulling a wagon
- Pushing heavy boxes

- Squeezing a stress ball
- Using a jump rope
- Using a therapy band
- Working with clay

Touch is the third large "powerhouse" of the sensory system.[95] This system helps the student understand bodily boundaries and appropriately respond to threats in the environment. Some strategies to target regulation in this area include:

- Deep squeezes
- Fidgets
- Lotions

- Pet therapy
- Soft blankets or pillows
- Weighed items (snake, lap band, hug seats)

The research suggests the use of these strategies can have the effects of building student-teacher relationships and helping the child expand their window of tolerance.[96] For example, if Jacob has a hard time sitting still and reacting calmly to feedback during math class, consider offering him a break, during which he can deliver a heavy item to the front office before class. This sensory break may help reset his system a bit to allow for increased tolerance and grit for the following activity.

USE MOVEMENT BREAKS

All students need movement and some need to move a LOT. You can be proactive in building in movement breaks for your students. The types and frequency of

---

95 Champagne, "Sensory Modulation."
96 Champagne, "Sensory Modulation."

movement will depend on the developmental level of your students and their individual needs. We recommend building in some level of movement breaks for your whole class and then consider providing some movement provisions for individual students as well. We know that recess is essential. Some states have recognized this with extended recess opportunities or have added second recess sessions for some grades. Whether this is the case for your school or not, you can add in some movement opportunities within the classroom. One approach for younger students is video-prompted dance routines. You can find many options online. Younger learners generally love dance parties that last for several minutes. Other teachers may engage in stretching or yoga routines. We even think that taking the whole class for walks to the bathroom, if you have taught and practiced your transitions, can be a way to get everybody up and moving.

For individual students who require movement, there are many ways to fulfill this need. Adaptive seating, like the use of wiggle cushions or therapy ball seats and stools that have some sway to them can be helpful; just be sure to teach how they are to be used. Standing desks also offer promise for some students.

Also, it can be helpful to students to assign them specific tasks. You can offer them a classroom role like paper passer and collector so that they can move around. Just be clear with your expectations for their behavior when filling that role. Another method for students who don't need a high level of supervision is to have them deliver items to the office or another classroom. Often, we see teachers that will send an empty envelope back and forth, prearranged with the destination, of course, just to give their students a way to move around. There can be added benefits here as the student feels helpful and may also develop additional relationships with those to whom they deliver the items.

TAKE A MINDFUL MINUTE DURING TRANSITIONS

Mindfulness helps bring the individual to the present moment, rather than thinking about something that happened in the past or worrying about something that might happen in the future. You may wish to build a quick "mindful minute" into your classroom transitions or routines. Consider using this time to teach, model, and practice a quick breathing exercise. There are countless ways to accomplish this task using music, body scanning techniques, meditation apps, yoga movements, etc. Many interoception (body awareness and body scanning) activities are also available online for use in a whole group, classroom setting.

MINDFULNESS MINUTES

Do you have any transitions or routines into which you'd like to build a mindful minute? Take a minute to look at your calendar or add a reminder into your phone to cue this strategy.

TEACH APPROPRIATE WAYS TO ESCAPE OR GET ATTENTION

In Chapter 6 we talked about functions of behavior and functional thinking. Here we urge you to think about some ways for students to get those functional needs met by 1) providing a temporary escape from task demands or unwanted attention, 2) making tasks easier or less aversive, and 3) accessing adult attention. While our end goal for all students is for them to follow instructions and complete all of their work, some students will need some short-term alternatives to problem behaviors to get needs met. We already discussed creating a safe space as one important option to put in place for temporary escape. That said, you may want to create some other ways to give a brief escape. These can range from the use of sensory tools to providing ways to access motor movement. Many students already use activities like getting a drink, going to the restroom, or seeking to go to the nurse as ways to get a break or access movement or access adult attention.

Another option is to teach students to request help with academic or other tasks. Asking for help can fill a need to access adult attention and often makes tasks less aversive by providing adult assistance. This can foster resilience as it teaches the student skills to use in other environments and with other adults. Regardless of the method, should you employ these types of strategies; they will need to be taught, modeled, and practiced when times are good. You can teach them to the whole class or to individual students. You can remind students of these options ahead of difficult routines and neutrally prompt them in the moment.

CONSIDER THE USE OF BREAK CARDS OR HELP CARDS

The use of break and help cards in place of or in combination with verbal requests may be helpful for students with language delays or for those who have difficulties communicating when frustrated. Help cards may simply say "help" on them or show a picture of a student raising their hand. Break cards might say "break" or "chill" or show a picture of a student appropriately taking a break.

Some teachers use a break card that has a few options of break activities to choose from (drink of water, deep breaths in the chill zone, go for a walk, etc.). You can get creative here. The cards can be placed or Velcroed to the student's desk. Some students may be able to keep the cards with them during the school day. For some students, you may wish to limit the number of break or help cards that they can use per day. You can decrease this number over time. For students on behavioral plans with individual reinforcement systems, it is often a good strategy to provide additional reinforcement for unused cards, thus encouraging their use sparingly, while providing ample opportunities for breaks or help on tougher days.

✓CHAPTER CHECKLIST
Support Individual Needs

❑ Provide additional wait time.

❑ Provide choices.

❑ Provide sensory tools.

❑ Use movement breaks.

❑ Take a mindful minute during transitions.

❑ Teach appropriate ways to escape or get attention.

❑ Consider the use of break cards, help cards, etc.

PART FIVE
REACTIVE STRATEGIES

CHAPTER 14

NOTICE AND RECOGNIZE TRIGGERS AND SIGNALS

In previous chapters, we described many proactive strategies that can greatly minimize a student's need to engage in disruptive or unsafe behaviors. When students are feeling safe and connected due to environmental supports, they are less likely to be triggered into an emotional or survival state outside their window of tolerance. However, we know that there are many uncontrolled factors in students' lives outside of school and unforeseen variables at school; problem behaviors and emotional reactions are still going to happen. The next few chapters review some trauma-sensitive ways to offer support for instances of agitation and to respond to and correct problem behaviors in the school setting.

Before we cover correcting behavioral errors, we need to recognize that students may become triggered by a reminder of a past experience, may be suffering from current traumatic experiences, or may just be experiencing temporary stressors.

It is important for you to be able to recognize both triggers (environmental events) and the signals (changes in student behavior) that can result from those triggers. How you initially respond is often the crucial difference between having a few difficult moments or a significant behavioral incident and a tough day for you and the student.

LEARN STUDENT TRIGGERS

There are a myriad of possible environmental events that can trigger students and they will be idiosyncratic to each individual. One way to organize your thoughts about triggers is to consider those that are fast triggers (antecedents) as opposed to slow triggers (setting events). Fast triggers will cause an immediate or nearly immediate behavioral or emotional reaction. Slow triggers are events that take place earlier and set the stage for fast triggers. It may be helpful to think of slow triggers as adding stress and fast triggers as the straw that broke the camel's back. Slow triggers can happen in the hours or days leading up to a behavioral or emotional reaction and are often more difficult to detect than fast triggers. You may be able to discover slow triggers for your students as you get to know them, and also through collaboration with caregivers outside of school.

Recognizing both fast and slow triggers is important as they both highlight opportunities to support students. For fast triggers, we will share potential supports to use in the moment. You can also look to eliminate fast triggers or ameliorate their impact. For slow triggers, some of the same supports may help in the moment, but you may want to use a team approach to address setting events or be prepared to adapt the student's school day on an as-needed basis. For example, if you know that missed medication is a slow trigger, you may work with the school team and the student's caregivers to get medication to the nurse's office to be administered at school. If you learn that arriving late to school or missing breakfast is a slow trigger, you might ensure that your student checks in with a staff member to ease them into the school day or to simply get that student a snack before entering the classroom.

COMMON TRIGGERS LIST

Common "Fast Triggers" (Antecedents):

- Being told no
- Change in schedule
- Correction on assignment
- Down time
- End of preferred activity
- Feedback on behaviors
- Fire drill
- Loud noises
- New adult in classroom
- Preferred item removed
- Proximity to peers
- Smell, sound, or sight connected with a traumatic experience
- Task or academic demand
- Teasing from peers
- Timer goes off
- Touch
- Transition

Common "Slow Triggers" (Setting Events/History):

- Allergies
- Change in routine
- Conflict on the walk to school
- Custody changes
- Fatigue
- Homelessness
- Hunger
- Illness
- Late to school
- Medication changes/missed medication
- Playground trouble before class
- Problems on the bus
- Sibling conflict
- Sleeping arrangements/sleep disturbance
- Social events or parties
- Traumatic incident
- Undiagnosed medical needs/pain

Think about your students and the types of things that tend to trigger an emotional or survival state response for them. Take a minute to make a quick list of fast or slow triggers you have observed.

LEARN STUDENT SIGNALS

You may see the term signals or precursor behaviors used to describe the signs of agitation or other difficulties that students show early on in a cycle of behavioral escalation. Some students may show predictable patterns with their signals, while others' signals may be more like isolated events. Jon has worked with many students who show reliable precursor behaviors as signs of agitation and as precursors to serious behavior issues. One memorable student would groan and rub his pencil on the edge of his desk before progressing to a temper tantrum. Once his team recognized this pattern, his teacher was able to intervene early. Prompting this student to ask for help or a break, as a replacement behavior for having a tantrum, worked to manage his frustration in the moment.

COMMON SIGNALS LIST

Common "Signals" (Precursor Behaviors):

- » Change in breathing
- » Grunting
- » Laughter
- » Less eye contact/hiding
- » Less talking/withdrawal
- » Looking away, turning body away
- » More eye contact/glaring
- » More talking/anxious chatter
- » No response
- » Pacing
- » Pushing materials away
- » Self-stimulating behaviors, flapping
- » Standing up
- » Tapping pencil

In the next chapter, we will share some potential responses for you to use in the classroom when you suspect your student has experienced triggering events or when you suspect that they are showing signals of behavior escalation. You need to consider what approaches are a good fit for your classroom culture and for individual students.

DETECTING SIGNALS

What types of signals of agitation do you observe in your students? Making a list can help you remember that these are behaviors that you may respond to with one of the strategies discussed in the next few chapters.

CHAPTER 15

RESPOND TO TRIGGERS AND SIGNALS

Now that you have a better grasp on recognizing environment triggers and behavioral signals, we want to prepare you with a variety of ways to respond to these changes.

PROMPT A MOVEMENT ACTIVITY OR RHYTHMIC ACTIVITY

For some students and adults, movement is simply a need. It can be more of a need when stressed, triggered, or otherwise dysregulated. You may want to consider making regular movement breaks a practice for all students, but also look to prompt students to access movement as needed. There is some evidence that students with trauma exposure can regain some level of regulation when they engage in more rhythmic movements, such as passing a ball back and forth with an adult or peer.[97] One approach to consider here is the tried-and-true method of asking your student to deliver something for you, provided it is safe to send the student on an errand at that time. Jon has had success with simply directing a student to do a number of jumping jacks or push-ups. If this support appears to be helpful, you can challenge your student to see how many they can do in one minute. As an experiment, next time you are stressed, try engaging in one minute of intensive exercise and see if you feel a reset.

Teachers have successfully set up mini movement courses for students in the classroom or in the hallway. Typically, there are visual prompts for a series of movements that have been pre-taught. For example, students can be instructed to do push-ups against the wall, hop on one foot through a hopscotch course, spin in a circle three times, etc. You can prompt a number of circuits through a movement course for your students. Some students may respond well to the rhythmic activity of using a rocking chair. If it is not disruptive to the rest of your class, you could direct individual students to follow along with dance or movement videos. Overall, these types of movement activities can help with regulation, while also allowing a brief break from any triggering stimuli.

PROVIDE PASSIVE ACTIVITIES

For some students, providing or prompting a passive activity can be helpful when you detect signals or triggering events. Passive activities can take many forms such as going to the safe space in your classroom, being given time to read, or listening to a story. In addition to prompting them in the moment, and depending on the needs of your students, you may want to consider class-wide passive activities following transitions from more active routines like P.E. or recess. For example, listening to a story might be a calming, class-wide reset prior to engaging in academic lessons.

---

97   van der Kolk, *The Body Keeps Score*, 90.

PROMPT INDEPENDENT ACTIVITIES OR BREAKS

Independent activities or breaks also give students an alternative to an activity that may be triggering or stressful, but are typically applied to individuals only as needed or on a prescribed schedule, rather than as a class-wide routine. For some students, you may want to prompt a break in the classroom safe space without instructing them to perform an activity. For other students, you will want to direct them to engage in an activity or offer a choice in activities. Directing your student to do a specific activity is especially important if you suspect they may be accessing a break as a means of escape from academic demands. Pre-teach how to engage in each activity to help ensure that your student transitions well and that the activity routine is successful in helping your student to regulate.

One experienced teacher that Jon works with supports several classrooms of students with significant behavioral and emotional needs. She teaches each student six calming activities at the start of the school year and then teaches the strategies to each new student who enrolls during the school year. When it is time for an activity break, the student rolls two foam dice and then chooses between the two numbers that correspond to the pre-taught activities. This technique ensures that the students know what to do when prompted to choose an activity break. This approach also harnesses the power of providing choice in helping ensure compliance with expectations for the break routine.

USE PROXIMITY

As discussed in Chapter 11, your use of proximity to students and the placement of your body can be powerful support techniques. When you see students displaying signals of agitation or when triggering events are suspected, moving closer to them often prevents behavioral escalation. For instance, if teasing is a trigger for one of your students and you suspect this is beginning, simply moving toward or between the two students involved may be enough for the triggered student to feel supported. This also serves as a deterrent to the potential offending student. You can debrief with either or both later, but simply using your proximity may allow instruction to continue for all in the moment. When supporting vulnerable students in the classroom, Jon has often positioned his body to shield the vulnerable student from potential triggering students. Especially if a relationship has been built, this conveys support to your student without drawing undo attention to the situation; adding a covert thumbs up or a knowing look can cement that support.

Sometimes using our proximity to get closer to students to offer support is the right technique, while sometimes this may unintentionally escalate a student. If getting closer to your student following the observation appears to escalate your student, move away and try to position yourself out of their personal space and at a front-side angle. Now is the time to think about the safety of your other students. If there is significant behavioral escalation, this may be time for a room clear.

PROMPT AND ALLOW PREFERRED ACTIVITIES

Upon observing signals of agitation, especially if the situation appears significant or is escalating quickly, prompting a preferred activity can be a helpful tool to prevent significant behavioral problems. This activity can be anything the student enjoys and that you find acceptable for your classroom. We caution you to use this approach sparingly and to watch for patterns with this technique. Students can begin to use their signals or other forms of behavioral escalation to access preferred activities. If you suspect such a pattern, work with your school support staff who have behavioral expertise as it may be time for a Functional Behavior Assessment (FBA) and an individual Behavior Intervention Plan (BIP).

SHOW CONFIDENCE AND GIVE EXTRA TIME

Giving confidence while allowing extra time can be a great approach when students may be triggered by difficult tasks and when they show signals of agitation surrounding these tasks. As with most interactions, showing confidence is more effective as relationships deepen, however this can also help to build relationships. Giving extra time can help decrease the impact of academic or task triggers. When combining these approaches, you may be able to get your student through some difficult routines. Think of this as lending your calm to allow the student to potentially choose a strategy or increase their window of tolerance.

ISSUE CHOICE

Proactively issue choice for some students during difficult routines and also on an as-needed basis. There are many ways to offer choice, but when applied to students who are showing signals of agitation, it is best to avoid a choice between complying or choosing a punishing option (e.g., "You can complete this now or lose your recess to finish your work"). This type of choice has its place, but it can escalate an agitated student. For your students that who triggered and showing signals of agitation, only use choices that give them some options to self-regulate. Some examples might be giving options of where to sit, what materials to use, what topic to write about, or in what order to complete tasks. All of these choices allow you to maintain some instructional control as learning will still be occurring. Being given choice can help de-escalate and self-regulate a wide range of students.

HELP FOCUS, GET STARTED ON TASK

To help a student focus and get started with a task, consider nonverbal or verbal prompting. If subtle prompting does not work, you can check for understanding of directions or ask if help is needed. Sometimes it may be best to help a student get started by modeling how the task is done or by starting the task for them. For example, you may write a sentence stem for the student or complete the first math problem for them. You can then prompt them to keep going and direct them to raise their hand when finished with the task, or you can just circle back to the student to check in and offer support and encouragement. At times, if a student is really struggling to initiate or maintain focus on academic tasks, you may want to use an "I do, you do" technique where you complete one problem or chunk of work and then prompt the student to do the next and repeat.

APPROACH WITH EMPATHY

In Chapter 6 we discussed approaching students with an empathetic approach. It is also an important approach to consider using when students have shown you signs of frustration. When you see signals of agitation, you should assume that behavioral escalation has already begun. Your response at this time can be crucial in determining if behavior will escalate further. To approach with empathy assumes positive intent and that your student wants to do well but is having difficulty. It will vary by the developmental level of your student, but key to approaching with empathy is to offer help either by labeling what you see (e.g., frustration) and prompting an alternative, issuing choice, or asking an open-ended question about what kind of help the student needs at the moment.

PROMPT HIGH-PROBABILITY REQUESTS/ BEHAVIORAL MOMENTUM

Another technique applicable to students who may have shut down is to use behavioral momentum. Behavioral momentum involves regaining instructional control by first issuing a high-probability request—one that the student is very likely to follow. If you get compliance with that first request, issue praise, and then move on to a more difficult request or task. If the student fails to comply, give wait time, and try a different directive. Jon at times has simply directed a student to wait where they are for a minute. In a sense, the student is complying by doing nothing at all and you can still use praise or show approval after a pause. Behavioral momentum works because once the student follows one direction, they are more likely to comply with the next one. We will explore the use of this technique further in the next chapter.

PROMPT A BREATHING STRATEGY

In Chapter 9, we reviewed the practice of teaching breathing strategies. Prompting these strategies, especially if previously taught and practiced, can be a useful support to students experiencing difficulty. Joining your student in the same breathing technique can be an additional support in promoting co-regulation. These are strategies that we use ourselves when experiencing stressful situations, both in the workplace and in other parts of our lives. Sometimes deeply breathing in and breathing out is enough to begin redirecting ourselves or others towards mindfulness and self-regulation. A quick refocus on the breath can expand windows of tolerance and help you move out of an emotional or survival state.

USE LESS LANGUAGE

We know that when students are escalated, they tend to lose some ability to process language. It should be no surprise that a technique to use when observing suspected triggers and signals is to cut down on our use of language. Language-heavy redirections are not only less likely to be effective; they may be counterproductive and lead to behavioral escalation. For some students, if you talk too much, you may run the risk of accidentally reinforcing low-level problem behaviors by applying adult attention. Consider using very short verbal directives and redirections. For example, if you were to issue a choice to a student showing signals of escalation, avoid rationale or processing and simply say something like, "You can sit here or at the table, you choose." For some students, this is also the time to consider nonverbal prompting.

GIVE EXTRA WAIT TIME

Closely related to the rationale for using less language, giving extra wait time can help agitated students appropriately respond or make a decision. If your student has any language-processing difficulties or is frustrated at the moment, giving wait time will help prevent further escalation and help ensure you get a favorable response. We like to combine giving wait time with issuing choice. It can be helpful to remove your attention while giving wait time. With older students, Jon will often tell the students, "I am going to give you a minute," while directing attention to students who are currently meeting expectations before circling back to the agitated student.

CONSIDER A ROOM CLEAR PROCEDURE

As we discussed in Chapter 7, a room clear procedure may be used effectively as a reactive strategy when needed. We recommend using this technique as an emergency response and only when the safety of your students or staff is a significant concern. On rare occasions you may consider a room clear if you cannot get an escalated student to leave the room and de-escalation does not appear to be likely with an audience of peers present. If room clear use becomes a pattern, it is time to use your support team and to consider FBA and BIP procedures. Your team will want to rule out the functions of escaping task demands or peer attention and accessing adult attention if the room clear procedure is needed repeatedly for any individual students.

REINTEGRATE STUDENTS BACK INTO ROUTINES AS SOON AS POSSIBLE

Reintegrating students after more serious behavioral problems can be difficult. There is a human tendency to want some type of consequences for rule-breaking offenses. For many of us, consequences mean punishment. We have empathy for teachers in this regard, especially when the student has had chronic behavioral concerns in the classroom. But what is more important than punishment, and how adults feel about punishment based on their cultural background, is that we achieve some change in behavior. To that end, it is generally acknowledged that we should reintegrate students back into the normal routine as soon as it is safe to do so. That does not mean there will not be consequences, but those consequences should be designed to change behavior.

We look to the disciplines of restorative justice for consequences that can change behavior while maintaining connections and relationships. The field of applied behavior analysis uses other approaches like overcorrection (having the student repeatedly engage in the expected behavior) and positive practice that offer the promise of behavioral instruction and rehearsal. We also want to highlight that getting back into the typical routine offers opportunities to provide positive reinforcement for meeting expectations and limits the potential reinforcing value of escaping task demands in the classroom. Remember that we have discussed how students will learn best when they feel safe and connected. Sitting in the principal's office is unlikely to help in this regard, while how you welcome your students back into your classroom can make a big difference in setting your students up for success.

✓CHAPTER CHECKLIST
Respond to Triggers and Signals

Here is a list of possible responses to triggers and signals for your reference:

- ❏ Prompt a movement activity or rhythmic activity.
- ❏ Provide passive activities.
- ❏ Prompt independent activities or breaks.
- ❏ Use proximity.
- ❏ Prompt and allow preferred activities.
- ❏ Show confidence and give extra time.
- ❏ Issue choice.
- ❏ Help focus, get started on tasks.
- ❏ Approach with empathy.
- ❏ Prompt high-probability requests/behavioral momentum.
- ❏ Prompt a breathing strategy.
- ❏ Use less language.
- ❏ Give extra wait time.
- ❏ Consider a room clear procedure.
- ❏ Reintegrate student back into routines as soon as possible.

CHAPTER 16

CORRECTING BEHAVIORAL ERRORS

It is our hope that you will treat behavioral errors much in the same way you treat academic errors; interrupt them, give some instruction or modeling, prompt the correct action, and then offer reinforcement or other feedback. When correcting behavioral errors, the hope is that beyond stopping the problem behavior, you work to limit the likelihood that those behaviors occur again in the future. You will also want to intervene in ways that do not escalate the situation or trigger or re-traumatize students. Here we offer some behavioral error-correction strategies and concepts that are often effective. It is very likely that you will make mistakes at times. After all of our years of experience, we still accidentally escalate a student or inadvertently reinforce a problem behavior. What is important is that you and your team can reflect and learn when that happens.

APPROACH WITH EMPATHY FIRST

We encourage you to approach students exhibiting difficulties with following directions or showing agitation with an empathetic approach first. This helps you avoid the fundamental attribution error (a natural tendency to ascribe the behavior of others to internal rather than external factors). An empathetic approach has the potential to maintain or further build trusting relationships with your students. When you see your students as individuals doing their best, your outlook of them tends to remain more positive than if you assume they are choosing to misbehave.

There are several ways to approach students with empathy first when you see them having difficulties with a particular task or if they are becoming agitated. For younger students or those who do not yet advocate well, you can approach, label the emotion they are displaying, and then prompt them to ask for assistance. For example, you might say, "Terrance, you look frustrated, ask me to move." This approach can work if you have a good idea of what might help Terrance. You can provide additional choices once you get to know your students better and understand what works best for them. For example, "Terrance, you look like you are having a tough moment. You can ask me to move or ask me to help you with your work." For older students, you might move to more open-ended questions like, "Terrance, what can I do to help you right now?" A key concept here is to start teaching your students to ask for what they need and hopefully to self-advocate.

CORRECT ERRORS PRIVATELY

In contrast to our previous discussion on the practice of praising or reinforcing appropriate behaviors publicly, we recommend a practice of reprimanding privately when feasible. If you cannot correct errors or reprimand in private, aim to deliver those behavioral corrections as covertly as possible and to keep those interactions brief. The rationale is that you do not want to teach students or signal their peers that a problem behavior is a way to access teacher attention or escape or delay task demands. An important exception is when the problem behavior is dangerous. If dangerous behavior occurs, such as physical aggression, then you want to get a handle on the situation as quickly as possible. In such cases, you might issue some public reprimands or otherwise draw attention to the problem behavior. In our experience, when you rarely issue public reprimands or raise your voice, in the event that you do need to do this to maintain safety, those redirections are more meaningful and get student attention much more effectively.

One way to correct errors or reprimand in private is to pause your reaction in the moment, perhaps issuing proximity reinforcement, and then ask the student making an error to step aside or outside. Do consider your knowledge of the student in deciding when to take this approach. If that student is likely to be defiant following your directive to step outside, then you now have another behavioral problem that may escalate into a power struggle. If you are concerned about defiance at this point, approach the student and issue your redirection or error correction as covertly as possible. Be careful about getting too close or crowding your student as this could trigger them into an emotional or physical reaction. In general, until you get to know your students, we recommend giving ample personal space.

PAUSE RESPONSES TO UNDANGEROUS BEHAVIORS

We have discussed how giving attention to undesired behaviors, even if reprimanding, can accidentally reinforce those behaviors, making them more likely to occur in the future. While there are some minor behaviors that you can choose to just ignore, providing you still reinforce appropriate behavior for the student, you will often need to correct minor behaviors so they do not persist or escalate. One way to decrease the reinforcing value of your attention when correcting errors is to pause your reactions. Recall that the concept of immediacy tells us that reinforcement is most effective right after or during the behavior. In instances where we need to respond, a pause has the potential to make that response less reinforcing. Pausing your reaction can also help ensure that you are keeping your calm so you can respond in a more systematic manner. It is our experience that with certain students, this is a very necessary practice, especially for those behaviors that you have recognized as potentially triggering an emotional reaction in yourself.

TEACH A ROOM CLEAR PROCEDURE

Consider using a room clear when a student's behavior escalates and there is a need to keep peers safe, or when the presence of peers might hamper de-escalation. It is important to pre-teach the room clear procedure as a classroom routine (teach, model, practice, and give feedback and reinforcement). Clearing your classroom will not be very efficient if students do not know what to do in a potentially heightened situation. We advise teaching the students a prompt to signal that it is time to leave the room. They will need to know how they are expected to line up and where. You will need to teach them whether they need to bring any items or to listen to the teacher for this information at the moment. For example, you might teach them to line up in the hallway outside the room with quiet voices. We recommend teaching students to refrain from making comments or staring; you can explain that sometimes being a good friend means respecting privacy if someone is upset. Minimizing peer attention can help avoid behavioral escalation. Students will need to know where to go and, if possible, this should be a consistent place. In our experience, the library or a spare classroom is a good destination.

As the teacher, you will want to be clear with your administration and other campus support staff on how to handle a room clear evacuation. We recommend having a procedure for obtaining help as you will need supervision for both the student experiencing difficulty and the students that have relocated. Often, other adults will work to de-escalate the student in the classroom while you supervise your relocated class. If you have a strong relationship with the escalated student, you may want to be the person to help with de-escalation. If you decide to put a room clear procedure into place, we suggest having some engaging academic work ready to take to the relocation destination. These can be tasks like word searches, other preferred worksheets, or a passive activity like reading a book to the class.

USE BEHAVIORAL MOMENTUM

Behavioral momentum is a favored technique of ours in cases where we need to assist with a student who is having significant difficulty, has shut down, or is unresponsive to typical prompting. Behavioral momentum starts with making a high-probability request. This request is one where the student is very likely to comply. We often think of the smallest, easiest, or most-preferred request we can make. The magic here is that once you get compliance with one directive, the student is more likely to comply with the next one. We advise very gradually increasing the difficulty of your requests, while giving praise for each successive instance of compliance.

For example, if a student became frustrated with an academic task, you might ask them to simply turn over their paper or close their laptop. You might then prompt the student to take a few deep breaths or get a drink of water. If the source of the student's agitation involved someone in the classroom, you might prompt them to take a walk before you get down to discussing the problem. If you are empathetic and acknowledge compliance along the way, you can often get back to the task at hand or to a place where the original behavior concern can be discussed.

USE LEAST TO MOST INTRUSIVE ERROR CORRECTION PROCEDURES

One important aspect of a supportive classroom, in addition to responding to triggers and signals, is to be prepared to correct behavioral errors in a systematic fashion. The best methods to use are those that minimize interruptions to instructions. A systematic approach allows adults to respond dispassionately. It helps you to keep your calm, and ultimately, your students to stay more regulated, when you respond with a system that is predictable and depersonalized.

Below we offer error-correction steps to consider, organized in a roughly least to most intrusive hierarchy. It is important to maintain consistency with any school-wide procedures in place, although you may work in some additional steps for individual students or certain populations. Lacking a school-wide system, consider using a series of least to most intrusive responses for your classroom, balancing how many redirection opportunities are appropriate prior to a discipline referral or involving the office. Depending on the developmental level of your students, consider teaching the error correction steps and posting them. Lastly, recognize what behaviors are dangerous and need a more immediate and intrusive response. Make sure you are well aware of safety or crisis plans for your school building.

Sample Least to Most Error Correction Continuum:

» Planned Ignoring (consciously ignore if safe, and pair with reinforcement when the student begins meeting expectations)

» Proximity/Vicarious Reinforcement (reinforce a close-by peer who is meeting expectations)

» Nonverbal Prompt/Gesture (eye gaze; point to task, item, or area; model hand raising)

» Verbal Prompt/State the Expectation (give wait time)

» Empathy/Offer Help (consider strategies introduced in Chapter 15; consider moving to this step if you notice signals or triggers)

» Issue Choice (give wait time)

» Issue a High-Probability Prompt (give wait time and build behavioral momentum if the student complies)

» Issue a Directive Prompt (use firm directive to try and gain control of an escalating situation; give wait time)

» Room Clear/Call for Assistance (keep everyone safe)

In the above continuum of least to most error correction responses, wait time is repeatedly mentioned. Pausing your reactions and giving wait time can be helpful in several ways, as we've previously outlined.

If you detect patterns of agitation where individual students respond reliably to triggers, consider systematically moving to offering help or to promoting some of the strategies introduced in Chapter 15. For all students, if you start to see trends of needing these supports or of frequently using an error correction continuum, consider taking some data to look for patterns. If problem behaviors are serious or persistent, collaborate with your support staff and consider FBA and BIP procedures.

ERROR CORRECTIION CONTINUUM

Consider your current error-correction procedures. Do you want to re-order your responses to problem behaviors in the classroom? Where could you add wait time or less intrusive strategies into your typical response patterns?

✓CHAPTER CHECKLIST
Correcting Behavioral Errors

❑ Approach with empathy first.

❑ Correct errors privately.

❑ Pause responses to undangerous behaviors.

❑ Teach a room clear procedure.

❑ Use behavior momentum.

❑ Use least to most intrusive error correction procedures.

CHAPTER 17

AVOID
RE-TRAUMATIZING

While you consider incorporating various strategies, try to avoid inadvertently re-traumatizing the student or adding adversity to their school experience. As much as possible, ensure your students are feeling safe and connected so they can learn.

Some important strategies covered in previous chapters to keep in mind include:

» Get on your student's level/height (avoid approaching from behind).

» Ask to enter student's space or touch their materials.

» Use less language.

» Use a calm voice and body language.

» Correct errors privately.

Related to private error correction, consider your methods of collecting homework and assignments. Avoid showing grades publicly or highlighting who did well and who failed. Consider ways of collecting homework discreetly so as not to publicly embarrass the student(s) who do not have it completed. When possible, offer space and time for students to complete homework at school. There are often many family and community variables related to homework completion over which the student has no control. Many students are in after-school care or other programs as their caregivers are often working multiple jobs. Other students have extended travel time on school buses or public transportation before and after school. Additionally, many of your students do not have their own rooms or quiet spaces in which to study or complete work in the home environment. A number of students miss school or cannot complete homework because they are responsible for caring for younger siblings. Have compassion for these potential variables; often you may not be aware of these situations.

Here are a few additional considerations to avoid re-traumatization while you are developing your classroom approaches.

PAY ATTENTION TO YOUR OWN STRESS LEVELS

First and foremost, continue to reflect on whether or not you are bringing calm into your classroom interactions, especially when students are escalated. If you are operating in survival or emotional mode, you are much more likely to trigger or even re-traumatize students. Go back to Chapter 5 and reflect on your practices to build your own calm and expand your window of tolerance as needed.

DON'T MAKE ASSUMPTIONS ABOUT "TRAUMA BEHAVIOR"

Even if you have students with known trauma exposure, you will not necessarily be able to predict their behaviors or educational outcomes. Don't make any assumptions about your students, just get to know them. Some students with an ACE (Adverse Childhood Experience) score of two struggle more in school than those with a score of eight. Each student has different resilience factors, coping skills, and ability levels. Also, just because a student appears to be functioning normally for a period of time doesn't mean that they will not demonstrate trauma symptoms at any time. Many children are able to "hold it together" for a period of time before they slip into a survival or emotional state. There is no one-size-fits-all formula or prediction for trauma exposure and symptom expression.

AVOID ASSUMPTIONS ABOUT FAMILY ARRANGEMENTS

Be considerate when referring to family and home situations. Do not assume that all of your students live with their biological parents in a single-family home. Many students live in multifamily or multigenerational homes. Others may be homeless. Students may live with one or more of their biological parents, foster parents, stepparents, extended family members, or a friend's family. Think back to our chapter on building relationships. It may be wise to gather information about family and home environments as you get to know your students. When in doubt, refer to "family" instead of "parents" when addressing your class, and learn more about each family's cultural and spiritual perspectives to increase sensitivity as you build relationships.

BE CONSIDERATE IN YOUR CURRICULUM CHOICES

At times, students who have previously experienced trauma become re-traumatized by homework assignments, activities, and assigned readings. In his own work with schools, the founder of the Equity Literacy Institute and EdChange, Paul C. Gorski, recognized the possibility of educators traumatizing and re-traumatizing students. He noticed that educators may glance over systemic injustices that some students face.[98] One injustice that educators may address is racism. Referring to it in the past tense can minimize your students' current experiences and potentially re-traumatize those who experience institutional, personal, and systemic racism. Educators are becoming increasingly aware of the ways that their school system is centered around outdated cultural norms and content. Some educators have used this refocus to find curriculum materials that

---

98   Gaffney, "When Schools Cause Trauma."

help to make classic materials relevant to modern populations to avoid further traumatization.

Our friends have recently experienced a different form of curricular re-traumatization personally. Years ago, they adopted extended family members after they were removed from an environment in which they were trauma-exposed. They recently noticed that the youngest girl had received a zero on a writing assignment in her fifth-grade class. After talking to her, they learned she had not completed the assignment, which was to write about the first two years of her life. The teacher wanted to learn more about her students and inspire them to write creatively about their own lives. However, this assignment triggered memories of early trauma for a student who did not have a positive association with adults during early life. When you are asking students to share personal stories, be sensitive to these potential triggers and offer choices for students to make based on comfort level. For example, in this situation, the writing prompt could have been to write about your own life or a particular time period of your choice.

Another factor to consider related to curriculum and trauma is the harm caused by "tracking" students or placing them into leveled groups or classes based on ability levels. Although the levels aren't usually explicitly stated, students quickly pick up on the intelligence and achievement levels of their peers. Considering our previous review of trauma symptoms, it is likely that many of your "slower" learners have slow progress that is primarily impacted by trauma. Sorting them into lower classes may further disillusion these students and re-traumatize them. As much as possible, avoid tracking groups of students into different groups or classes. Provide substantial evidence-based academic interventions for a student before recommending they move to a slower learning or lower-level class.

TRAUMA-SENSITIVE CURRICULUM

Consider your curriculum and whether the content and assignments are sensitive to students who have trauma exposure. What might you shift or change in your materials or content delivery?

AVOID CHANGING THE RULES OR ADDING NEW/UNEXPECTED CONSEQUENCES

As we've discussed, changes in the environment can easily trigger a response from the limbic system or brain stem outside of the window of tolerance. As much as possible, try to keep consistent rules in your classroom and avoid adding new or unexpected consequences. Do not escalate criteria as you are interacting with a child. For example, if you tell the student he can go to recess after answering three more questions on his worksheet, do not return to the desk and ask him to correct mistakes in those three problems unless your original instruction was that they needed to be completed correctly. Pick the battle of correcting mistakes after the incentive or consequence is earned. When you escalate the criteria or change the rules, a power struggle may occur, which can potentially lead to a significant behavioral response.

AVOID CREATING A SITUATION IN WHICH THE STUDENT IS CORNERED

Try to make sure the student is always able to make a choice that is appropriate and safe. When students feel cornered, either emotionally or physically, they are likely to react from a flight, flight, or freeze survival state. This reflects back to our conversation on coercion versus cooperation. Avoid using "or else" statements with students to protect them from feeling emotionally cornered. Avoid using your body to block students into a physical area or to crowd over their workspace to protect them from feeling physically cornered. Being aware of these variables will keep both you and the student safer.

AVOID PUNISHING TRAUMA RESPONSES

When educators overreact or punish students for behaviors that are trauma responses, they are likely to shrink the window of tolerance and receive a disruptive response. As much as possible, try to avoid sending students out of the learning environment as a consequence for their behaviors. When you attempt to discipline a child with suspension or expulsion, you reinforce his sense that adults aren't safe. When you can provide consistency and keep the student in the learning environment, returning him to class as soon as he is regulated, you build that safety and connection. This is how an individual is able to heal and expand their window of tolerance in order to learn coping skills and educational content.

It is incredibly common for schools to use disciplinary actions that focus on "responsibility" or individual "choices." In general, misbehavior is typically not a conscious or intentional choice from the student's rational brain.

When educators focus on enforcing school policies rather than helping the individual, it makes room for potentially triggering a student's trauma.[99] Some educators have stated that when we focus "on the idea that it's the students who need fixing rather than the systems, policies that focus disproportionately on student responsibility often sustain the same unjust structures that create trauma in the first place."[100] Blaming students for the systems they are part of is not only unfair and unreasonable, but likely alienating and even re-traumatizing for them. Consider the disciplinary consequences utilized in your classroom and school system, and think about whether they are working to support students and to teach skills that help them make better choices in the future. If you notice that the current practices don't necessarily work to support students' needs, consider changing your classroom consequences and advocating to leadership to change school-wide consequences. Reflect on the reactive and error-correction strategies we've covered in previous chapters for guidance.

DO NOT FORCE THE CHILD OR FAMILY TO TELL THE STORY

If a student begins to tell you about a past situation he witnessed at home or in the community, try to listen without judgment. If possible, provide a safe and neutral opportunity for the student to share concerns and worries with you. Never force a child to tell his story or explain past experiences to you. If the student chooses to tell you something traumatic, try to maintain a calm and open reaction. Avoid

---

99   Gaffney, "When Schools Cause Trauma."
100   Gaffney, "When Schools Cause Trauma."

statements such as "you're okay," or "you'll be fine." Instead, simply listen and reassure the student that you and the school are safe spaces.

Allow students to share pieces of their story with you within their comfort level. They might tell you a sentence then retract for months before sharing again. This pattern is common in individuals who have experienced trauma. Continue to lend your calm and provide consistency in your interactions with the student. It is easy to withdraw and think you are not getting anywhere, but the student may be testing you and seeing how you will react to their story.

Similarly, when a student tells one story about an incident and then retells the story differently another time, do not assume they are lying. It's possible their brain is just not connecting to the story in the same way and they do not have the same words or memories related to the experience. As we discussed in the early chapters, trauma is often not stored as a narrative in the brain, but rather segmented and imprinted on the body.

The more you understand typical trauma responses, the more you can help students and families accept their emotions and behaviors. You can normalize the reactions of the individuals involved with statements such as:

"This is okay and it is normal."

"Things are temporary and everything can change."

"These are very normal reactions to a difficult situation."

NEVER promise a student that you won't tell anyone what he or she is telling you. As educators and mandated reporters, we are required to report any suspicions of abuse and neglect to the appropriate state agencies. Seek further information about your local laws and regulations from your site administrator. Consider the other mental health professionals within the school and community, and consult with them when necessary.

AVOID PHYSICAL INTERVENTIONS

Dr. Bessel van der Kolk's book *The Body Keeps the Score* highlights the case of one young woman in a psychiatric ward who had a history of sexual abuse.[101] When her behaviors were deemed unsafe by staff members, they utilized physical restraint methods. Unknowingly, these physical restraints triggered flashbacks and sensations of being held down and raped. As much as possible, we need to avoid intervening physically or restraining students who have experienced trauma.

Please reference your district and state guidelines regarding the use of physical restraint and seclusion. ALWAYS follow these guidelines and use these methods as a very last resort.

RECONNECT AND DEBRIEF AFTER CRISES

Sometimes teachers become upset when, following a significant behavioral incident, a student is brought back to their room too soon or without further punishment. In that situation, it's important to consider the context of the problem behavior. If the students acted out when they were dysregulated, such as when they were shouting out in class or talking back, allow them back into the room when they are regulated.

If the student leaves the room to become regulated and returns to the class calmly, you need to allow the student back to the room and try to let it go. At that point, if you are not yet calm or ready to receive the child back in the room, request help or take your own break for regulation. As we've discussed at length, it is no surprise if you escalate along with the student, co-regulating into an emotional or survival state. Take a minute to use interoception or other calming strategies in order to continue with your instructional flow in a safe manner.

When everyone is back in a calm state, perhaps later in the day or even later in the week, consider taking some time to reconnect and debrief with the student. This practice can allow you to further build your relationship, hear the student's side of the story (if they have the skills to communicate), and co-regulate to expand

---

101   van der Kolk, *The Body Keeps Score*, 25.

each person's window of tolerance. We often see educators skipping this step, as it is difficult to find the time to spend one on one with a student, especially if that student triggered an emotional reaction in the adult. If necessary, focus on your self-care practices or reflect back to Chapter 8 on separating the deed from the doer to find something to like about the behavior. The oft-forgotten step of debriefing and reconnecting can make a big difference in breaking down a behavioral cycle and building a sense of safety and connection.

✓CHAPTER CHECKLIST
Avoid Re-Traumatizing

Here is a quick reminder of strategies to keep in mind to avoid re-traumatizing your students:

- ❏ Pay attention to your own stress levels.
- ❏ Don't make assumptions about "trauma behavior."
- ❏ Avoid assumptions about family arrangements.
- ❏ Be considerate in your curriculum choices.
- ❏ Avoid changing the rules or adding new/unexpected consequences.
- ❏ Avoid creating a situation in which the student is cornered.
- ❏ Avoid punishing trauma responses.
- ❏ Do not force the child or family to tell the story.
- ❏ Avoid physical interventions.
- ❏ Reconnect and debrief after crises.

CONCLUSION

Our hope is that you have gained some new knowledge and learned some new strategies from this book, and that you have refocused on your own wellness. When educators are able to build their own calm, we see amazing practices taking place in the classroom. If you find yourself becoming triggered by student or adult behaviors, pause and reflect on your own window of tolerance. When you are in a thinking state rather than an emotional or survival state, you will be much more effective in implementing proactive, consistent, and appropriate supports. As you build predictability, safety, and connection into your classroom routines, we hope you notice a shift in the energy and behavior of your students.

Remember that we tend to get more of what we give attention to. Direct your attention and use your voice to reinforce, prompt, and acknowledge what you want to see in your classroom. Try to set up your instructional space proactively and give yourself permission to reorganize your environment as you learn more about your students. Think about what practices are a good fit for *your* classroom and be prepared to respond to student difficulties with calming strategies and consistency. Remember the quote below; you are already well on your way to providing that island of safety for your students.

"The greatest hope for traumatized, abused, and neglected children is to receive a good education in schools where they are seen and known, where they learn to regulate themselves, and where they can develop a sense of agency. At their best, schools can function as islands of safety in a chaotic world."

—Dr. Bessel van der Kolk

APPENDIX

ADVERSE CHILDHOOD EXPERIENCES (ACEs) QUESTIONNAIRE[102]

FINDING YOUR ACE SCORE

While you were growing up, during your first 18 years of life:

1. Did a parent or other adult in the household often...   ❑ Yes ❑ No

Swear at you, insult you, put you down, or humiliate you?

or

Act in a way that made you afraid that you might be physically hurt?

2. Did a parent or other adult in the household often...   ❑ Yes ❑ No

Push, grab, slap, or throw something at you?

or

Ever hit you so hard that you had marks or were injured?

3. Did an adult or person at least 5 years older than you ever...   ❑ Yes   ❑ No

Touch or fondle you or have you touch their body in a sexual way?

or

Try to or actually have oral, anal, or vaginal sex with you?

4. Did you often feel that ...   ❑ Yes   ❑ No

No one in your family loved you or thought you were important or special?

or

Your family didn't look out for each other, feel close to each other, or support each other?

5. Did you often feel that...   ❑ Yes   ❑ No

You didn't have enough to eat, had to wear dirty clothes, and had no one to protect you?

or

Your parents were too drunk or high to take care of you or take you to the doctor if you needed it?

6. Were your parents ever separated or divorced?   ❑ Yes   ❑ No

7. Was your mother or stepmother: ❑ Yes   ❑ No

Often pushed, grabbed, slapped, or had something thrown at her?

or

Sometimes or often kicked, bitten, hit with a fist, or hit with something hard?

or

Ever repeatedly hit over at least a few minutes or threatened with a gun or knife?

8. Did you live with anyone who was a problem drinker or alcoholic or who used street drugs?   ❑ Yes   ❑ No

9. Was a household member depressed or mentally ill or did a ❑ Yes ❑ No
household member attempt suicide?

10. Did a household member go to prison? ❑ Yes ❑ No

Number of "Yes" answers: _____. This is your ACE Score.

BIBLIOGRAPHY

APA Presidential Task Force on Posttraumatic Stress Disorder and Trauma in Children and Adolescents. "Children and Trauma: Update for Mental Health Professionals." 2008. https://www.apa.org/pi/families/resources/update.pdf.

Blad, Evie, and Corey Mitchell. "Black Students Bear Uneven Brunt of Discipline, Data Show." *Education Week* 37, no. 29 (May 2018): 10. https://www.edweek.org/ew/articles/2018/05/02/black-students-bear-uneven-brunt-of-discipline.html.

Centers for Disease Control. "Adverse Childhood Experiences (ACEs)." Last modified April 2, 2019. https://www.cdc.gov/violenceprevention/childabuseandneglect/acestudy/index.html.

Champagne, Tina. "Webinar: Sensory Modulation & Mental Health." Pearson Clinical, Webinar recorded 2011. https://www.ot-innovations.com/webinar-sensory-modulation-mental-health.

Cherry, Kendra. "What Is the Negativity Bias?" *Very Well Mind.* Updated April 11, 2019. https://www.verywellmind.com/negative-bias-4589618.

Child Trends. "Adverse Childhood Experiences." March 7, 2019. https://www.childtrends.org/indicators/adverse-experiences.

Child Trends. "Children and Youth Experiencing Homelessness." May 8, 2019. https://www.childtrends.org/indicators/homeless-children-and-youth.

Conscious Discipline. "Chapter 9: Positive Intent." Accessed January 11, 2020. https://consciousdiscipline.com/free-resources/book-portal/chapter-9-positive-intent/#positiveintentsummary.

Conscious Discipline. "The Conscious Discipline Brain State Model." Accessed December 20, 2019. https://consciousdiscipline.com/methodology/brain-state-model.

Cook, Clayton R., Erin A. Grady, Anna C. Long, Tyler Renshaw, Robin S. Codding, Aria Fiat, and Madeline Larson. "Evaluating the Impact of Increasing General Education Teachers' Ratio of Positive-to-Negative Interactions on Students' Classroom Behavior." *Journal of Positive Behavior Interventions* 19, no. 2 (2017), 67–77.

Crisis Prevention Institute. "Trauma-Informed Care Resources Guide." 2017. https://educate.crisisprevention.com/Trauma-Informed-Care.html?code=BLIT01TICRG&src=Blog.

Dweck, Carol S. *Mindset: The New Psychology of Success*. New York: Ballantine Books, 2007.

Echo Training. "Resources." Accessed December 23, 2019. https://www.echotraining.org/resources.

Gaffney, Carrie. "When Schools Cause Trauma." *Teaching Tolerance* 62 (Summer 2019).

Gottman, John M., James Coan, Sybil Carrere, and Catherine Swanson. "Predicting Marital Happiness and Stability from Newlywed Interactions." *Journal of Marriage and Family* 60, no. 1 (February 1998): 5–22.

Government of South Australia. "Interoception." Department for Education. February 2019. https://www.education.sa.gov.au/supporting-students/health-e-safety-and-wellbeing/health-support-planning/managing-health-education-and-care/neurodiversity/interoception.

Griffin, Rick. "Trauma-Supportive Certification: Course Two." Lecture, Paradise Valley Unified School District, Phoenix, AZ, October 25, 2019.

Gunn, Jennifer. "Self-Care for Teachers of Traumatized Students," Resilient Educator. Accessed March 26, 2020. https://resilienteducator.com/classroom-resources/self-care-for-teachers.

Harvard Medical School. "Giving Thanks Can Make You Happier." *Healthbeat*. Accessed January 7, 2020. https://www.health.harvard.edu/healthbeat/giving-thanks-can-make-you-happier.

Haynes, Trevor. "Dopamine, Smartphones, and You: A Battle for Your Time," Harvard University. May 1, 2018. http://sitn.hms.harvard.edu/flash/2018/dopamine-smartphones-battle-time.

Kataoka, Sheryl, Audra Langley, Marleen Wong, Shilpa Baweja, and Bradley Stein. "Responding to Students with PTSD in Schools," *Child and Adolescent Psychiatric Clinics of North America* 21, no. 1 (January 2012): 119–33.

Khazan, Olga. "Inherited Trauma Shapes Your Health." *The Atlantic*. October 16, 2018. https://www.theatlantic.com/health/archive/2018/10/trauma-inherited-generations/573055.

Lee, Min-Sun, Juyoung Lee, Bum-Jin Park, Yoshifumi Mayazaki. "Interaction with Indoor Plants May Reduce Psychological and Physiological Stress by Suppressing Autonomic Nervous System Activity in Young Adults: A Randomized Crossover Study." *Journal of Physiological Anthropology* 34, no. 21 (April 28, 2015). https://jphysiolanthropol.biomed central.com/articles/10.1186/s40101-015-0060-8.

McKibben, Sarah. "The Two-Minute Relationship Builder." *ASCD Education Update* 56, no. 7 (July 2014). http://www.ascd.org/publications/newsletters/education_update/jul14/vol56/num07/The_Two-Minute_Relationship_Builder.aspx.

National Institute for the Clinical Application of Behavioral Medicine. "How to Help Your Clients Understand Their Window of Tolerance Infographic." Accessed December 23, 2019. https://www.nicabm.com/trauma-how-to-help-your-clients-understand-their-window-of-tolerance.

Perry, Bruce. "Maltreatment and the Developing Child: How Early Childhood Experience Shapes Child and Culture." The Margaret McCain Lecture Series. 2015. http://www.lfcc.on.ca/mccain/perry.pdf.

Pickens, Isaiah B., and Nicole Tschopp. *Trauma-Informed Classrooms*. Reno, NV: National Council of Juvenile and Family Court Judges (2017): 12.

Positive Behavioral Interventions and Supports. "Materials." Accessed January 7, 2020. https://www.pbis.org/resource-type/materials#bullying-prevention.

Singh, Nirbhay. "Mindfulness-Based Positive Behavior Support (MBPBS)." Accessed December 24, 2019. https://hcpbs.files.wordpress.com/2017/10/mindfulness-based-pbs.pdf.

Singh, Nirbhay, Giulio Lancioni, Alan Winton, Brian Karazsia, and Judy Singh. "Mindfulness Training for Teachers Changes the Behavior of Their Preschool Students." *Research in Human Development* 10, no. 3 (2013): 211–33. https://www.tandfonline.com/doi/abs/10.1080/15427609.2013.818484.

Sunada, Joyce. "The Ripple Effect of Teacher Wellness: Taking Time Out for Your Wellbeing," Thompson Books Webinar. Accessed December 24, 2019.

van der Kolk, Bessel. *The Body Keeps the Score: Brain, Mind, and Body in the Healing of Trauma*. New York: Penguin Books, 2015.

Van Parys, Erica. "The Neurosequential Model and Practical Applications." Second Annual Early Childhood Social-Emotional Conference Lecture. December 5, 2019.

Walker, Tim. "'I Didn't Know It Had a Name': Secondary Traumatic Stress and Educators." *NEA Today*. October 18, 2019. http://neatoday.org/2019/10/18/secondary-traumatic-stress.

Wardlow, Liane. "The Positive Results of Parent Communication: Teaching in a Digital Age." Pearson Education. December 2013. https://www.pearsoned.com/wp-content/uploads/DigitalAge_ParentCommunication_121113.pdf.

Williams, Florence. *The Nature Fix: Why Nature Makes Us Happier, Healthier, and More Creative*. New York: W. W. Norton, 2017.

Zenger, Jack, and Joseph Folkman, "The Ideal Praise-to-Criticism Ratio." *Harvard Business Review*. March 15, 2013. https://hbr.org/2013/03/the-ideal-praise-to-criticism.

RECOMMENDED READING

Bailey, Becky. *Conscious Discipline: Building Resilient Classrooms*.

Colvin, Geoff. *Defusing Disruptive Behavior in the Classroom*.

Colvin, Geoff, and Terrance M. Scott. *Managing the Cycle of Acting-Out in the Classroom*.

Office of Special Education Programs. *Supporting and Responding to Student Behavior: Evidence-Based Classroom Strategies for Teachers*.

Simonsen, Brandi, and Diane Myers. *Classwide Positive Behavior Interventions and Supports: A Guide to Proactive Classroom Management*.

INDEX

ACKNOWLEDGMENTS

We want to acknowledge and recognize that nothing we have done professionally would be possible without the support of the educators who helped guide us as youths and continue to guide us as adults. In preschool through graduate school, we each had multiple teachers and education professionals who helped us realize a hopeful future. Teachers who stand tall in our memories are the ones who went the extra mile to build a connection or a relationship with us, regardless of the academic content they provided. We continue to benefit and learn from the leadership, expertise, modeling, and grace of educators with whom we now work. The majority of the content in this book is attributed to the privilege we've had working with and observing master educators in our careers. Thank you all for your patience, professionalism, and compassion over the years.

ABOUT THE AUTHOR

Laura Anderson, PsyS, is a school psychologist in Phoenix, Arizona. Her background includes school psychology positions in preschool through middle school, with a focus on advocating for students with significant behavioral needs and the staff who support them. Laura spends a considerable amount of her professional time training other educational professionals on behavioral practices and de-escalation strategies. Her professional passions include early intervention, staff wellness and self-care, and proactive behavioral systems. Laura is primarily focused on using effective collaboration between adults to facilitate the implementation of practical, evidence-based strategies.

Jon Bowen, M.A., is a school psychologist and positive behavioral support consultant with two decades of experience in diverse school settings. A major focus of Jon's work has been to create environments that are supportive of all students. Jon has taught at the college level and frequently provides professional development training and consultation for school staff related to proactive behavioral supports. Jon has a particular passion for supporting the educational professionals who care for our most challenged learners. Having had the privilege to work in hundreds of classrooms and to have learned from a myriad of fellow educators, Jon understands the value of best practices that are practical to implement.

Jon and Laura are married and live and work in Phoenix, Arizona. When they are not pursuing professional or continuing education endeavors, you are likely to find them catching live music or escaping to the wilderness.

For additional resources, or to contact the authors, please visit: www.the supportiveclassroom.com